Men
of the
Bible

*Fifty Biographical Sketches
of Biblical Men*

Dan Harmon

A Barbour Book

© MCMXCVII by Barbour & Company, Inc.

ISBN 1-55748-957-2

Published by Barbour & Company, Inc.
P.O. Box 719
Uhrichsville, Ohio 44683
http://www.barbourbooks.com

ecpa Member of the
Evangelical Christian
Publishers Association

Printed in the United States of America.

AARON
Exodus, Leviticus, Numbers, and Deuteronomy

When God commanded Moses to lead the Hebrews out of Egypt, Moses begged to be excused. "I am not an eloquent speaker," he complained. So God allowed Moses to engage his older brother Aaron to be his spokesman. So Aaron transmitted to the people God's words to Moses.

Moses and Aaron's encounters with Pharaoh in which God demanded, "Let My people go," are among the most dramatic portions of Scripture. They provide riveting lessons in divine patience and punishment. God performed astonishing miracles through Moses and Aaron—such as turning a stick into a snake and changing the Nile River into blood. God sent a string of catastrophes upon the Egyptians which culminated in the historic night when death visited the firstborn son of every Egyptian household. Still Pharaoh refused to release Israel or respect their God. Aaron is not always mentioned in the narrative of the Bible, but he was always at Moses' side.

The Exodus of Israel climaxed with their passage through the Red Sea and God's annihilation of the Egyptian army who had stubbornly followed them. Then, years passed when Israel wandered in the wilderness and sorely tried the patience of Moses and Aaron. As leaders, they did as the Lord commanded, but the people repeatedly lost faith. When thirsty or hungry or facing a hostile army, the Hebrews complained bitterly. Yet God met their needs in miraculous ways. One would think the wandering Hebrews, more than any other people in history, would have believed because they repeatedly saw God's power and faithfulness—yet they doubted and rebelled against their leaders.

Aaron was also given a task beyond that of spokesman. God made him the high priest and instructed that he be lavishly and meticulously attired for this position. Only Aaron and his descendants were authorized to offer sacrifices for the Israelites. Yet even Aaron lost faith. On one occasion, when Moses was alone on Mount Sinai for an extended period with the Lord, the people became restless and persuaded Aaron to make for them the image of a god. So Aaron melted gold into a calf-shaped idol for the people to worship. They believed it was the god that had brought them out of Egypt!

This misplaced allegiance and loss of control led to bloodshed and Moses had to intercede before the Lord on behalf of the people. In response, God forgave them and promised to remain with Israel. But because of Aaron's flawed leadership and the people's diminished respect for God as a result, God did not allow Aaron to enter the promised land.

When the time came for Aaron to die, the Lord instructed Moses to go with his brother to the top of Mount Hor. There Moses removed Aaron's beautiful robe and placed it on Aaron's son Eleazar, thus designating him as the next high priest. Aaron died and the Israelites spent thirty days in mourning for their leader and high priest.

ABIMELECH
Genesis 20

The Hebrew woman Sarah was very beautiful and Abimelech, king of Gerar, took notice. She had been living in Abimelech's country with Abraham for some time. Abimelech thought they were brother and sister and so brought Sarah into his household to be one of his wives, as was the accepted custom of the time. But Abimelech was a God-fearing man. He was devastated when the Lord came to him in a dream and revealed that Sarah was in fact Abraham's wife!

"But I did not know I was doing wrong!" Abimelech protested. "They both told me they were brother and sister."

Happily, the Lord had not allowed Abimelech to touch Sarah after she had entered his house. "Return Abraham's wife to him," the Lord said. "He is a prophet, and he will pray for you. But if you do not return her, you and everyone in your household will die."

Early the next day, Abimelech told his servants what had happened. He summoned Abraham and demanded to know why the couple had deceived him. Abraham explained: When he and Sarah entered Gerar he was not sure it was a land of God-fearing people. He was afraid some man enticed by Sarah's beauty would kill him in order to obtain her as a wife. So Abraham persuaded Sarah to pose as his sister. She was, after all, his half-sister because they had the same father.

Rather than venting his fury against Abraham, Abimelech

gave him an offering of livestock, slaves, and money. He gave him the best land in Gerar on which to live. Of course he returned Sarah to him unharmed. Abimelech wanted everyone to know he had not come near Sarah. During the time Sarah was in Abimelech's household the Lord had made the king impotent. But after Abraham prayed for him, God restored Abimelech to full health.

Abimelech is a notable example of a God-fearing man who, when confronted with his mistake, went out of his way to seek reconciliation with the people he had harmed and, most importantly, reconciliation with the Lord.

ABRAHAM
Genesis 11:27-25:10

Generally regarded as the "father of the Jewish nation," Abraham's life is a wondrous example of how God works His will in impossible situations.

The life story of this grand Old Testament patriarch would pale the most intricate plots of Hollywood screenwriters—and it all really happened! God told Abraham to break away from his father's family and go to a new land. God promised to make a great nation of Abraham's descendants and bless them. "I will bless those who bless you, and curse those who harm you," the Lord told him. So began the formation and trials of God's chosen people.

There was an unhappy chasm between Abraham and his nephew Lot. But when Lot and his household was captured by a warring kingdom, Abraham and a commando force of 300 soldiers rescued them. God made a covenant with Abraham and promised that his descendants would be as numerous as the stars in the sky—even though Abraham's wife Sarah was too old to bear children. In fulfillment of this promise God gave them a son in their old age. They named him Isaac.

Nowhere was Abraham's obedience so severely tested as in the mountains of Moriah where the Lord commanded him to sacrifice Isaac. Abraham prepared the altar, gathered the wood, lit the fire, bound the unsuspecting youth, and placed him on the altar. Abraham drew a knife and was actually poised to kill his son—so committed was he to God—when an angel of the Lord stayed his hand at the last instant.

Abraham had proven he would keep nothing from the Almighty, not even his cherished son. In return, God reiterated his pledge to make Abraham's descendants as numerous as the stars in the sky and as the grains of sand along the ocean shore.

Sarah lived to be 127, Abraham, 175, and they were buried in a cave in the field of Ephron in Canaan.

ADAM
Genesis 2:4-5:5

Adam was the first human, formed from dust and given God's own breath of life. He was placed in a beautiful garden God had planted in Eden. The Lord made Adam the caretaker of his garden and surrounded him with many wonderful plants for beauty and for food. God brought to Adam all the animals he had created, and Adam named them. Adam was free to enjoy this lovely garden. Only one restriction was placed on him: "Do not eat from the tree of the knowledge of good and evil," God warned. This tree was at the center of the garden.

God did not want Adam to live alone, so he put the man into a deep sleep, removed one of his ribs, and created a woman from the rib. He made the woman Adam's wife. Adam named her Eve.

Sadly Adam and Eve were persuaded by the serpent to eat fruit from the forbidden tree. This may be the most famous story in the Bible. It resulted in alienation between God and Adam and Eve and all their descendants. Adam and Eve were evicted from the garden and had to work the soil to grow their food.

This first sin led to the avalanche of sin that characterizes the whole human race. In fact, Adam and Eve's son Cain jealously murdered his own brother. Soon the world was so wicked the Lord was compelled to destroy it with a great flood. God allowed humanity to continue by preserving Noah and his family, but their descendants quickly returned to the errant ways established by Adam and Eve. It would take the crucifixion of Jesus Christ many centuries later to atone for Adam's original sin.

AMOS
Amos

"The Lord roars out of Zion. . . ."

So begins the prophecy of Amos, a sheep breeder and keeper of fig trees in Tekoa, a town in the land of Judah. God told him to leave this work and preach to the people of Bethel in Israel. Amos obeyed.

His message was indeed a roar. Amos began by proclaiming the Lord's judgment against the neighboring nations of Syria, Philistia, Phoenicia, Edom, Ammon, Moab, and Judah. He then declared God's wrath against Israel for a long litany of offenses. Amos particularly cited the rich who mistreated the poor and those who worshipped lifeless idols.

"Return to Me and you will live," he told the Israelites. Amos promised a coming day of doom, but concluded with the Lord's pledge to rebuild the fallen kingdom.

Amos is among the twelve minor prophets of the Old Testament and was the first biblical writer to teach that God rules the entire universe.

BALAAM
Numbers 22:5-24:25

God's sacred book, the Bible, occasionally contains true humor ranging from Old Testament foibles to the exaggerated illustrations used by Christ himself. (Envision a camel passing through the eye of a needle!)

Here is Balaam, a soothsayer from Mesopotamia, riding his donkey to visit King Balak of Moab. King Balak has a problem: The Israelites, wandering from Egypt to the Promised Land have arrived at the Jordan River and Balak sees them as a threat to his kingdom. They are God's chosen people and have already conquered entire armies. Balak does not want to fight them; he knows the Israelites are too strong. Yet if they remain in his territory, Balak fears they will consume everything in sight. They must be driven away.

Balak has a solution: Summon Balaam and have this Gentile prophet place a curse on the Israelites. He does so and promises Balaam a handsome reward.

Balaam wrestles with this proposal. When the Lord tells him plainly that the Israelites have God's own blessing, Balaam dutifully refuses Balak's request. "How can I curse what the Lord has blessed?" he reasons. Balak persists, and God permits Balaam to go to the king. "But do only what I tell you to do," the Lord commands. The Lord wants to impress upon Balaam his unhappiness with Balak's proposal and the importance of Balaam's strict obedience in this situation. The fact that God chooses to do this is memorable.

On the way to Moab, Balaam receives a sequence of rude surprises by his donkey. First the animal suddenly leaves the road and carries him into a field. Later, the donkey brushes against a stone wall, scraping Balaam's foot. Then the donkey lies down and refuses to move. Each time, Balaam angrily beats the poor creature. What Balaam has failed to see is that on each occasion, the donkey has been halted by an angel with a sword. Finally, Balaam gets the greatest surprise of all: The donkey looks at him and speaks!

"Why are you beating me?" asks the donkey.

"Because you embarrassed me," rebukes the astonished rider. "If I had a sword, I would kill you."

"Have I ever acted this way before?" challenges the donkey.

Upon reflection, Balaam has to admit, "No."

While the distracted diviner is discoursing with his donkey in what is perhaps the most hilarious scene in the entire Bible, the Lord reveals the angel to him. The awestruck traveler bows to his knees, apologizes for beating his frightened donkey, and offers to return home, if God so desires. The angel instructs Balaam to proceed to Moab, but reminds him to say exactly what the Lord tells him to say.

Balaam follows God's bidding and instead of cursing the Israelites, he blesses them three times, to King Balak's chagrin. The king sends Balaam away, thinking him a fool for squandering the chance to earn a king's reward. But Balaam corrects him: "Even if you offered me a house full of money, I could not disobey the Lord." These are bold words to say to an angry king! But in the wake of his experience with the donkey, Balaam understood very clearly who was the true King.

BARABBAS
Matthew 27:15-26; Mark 15:6-15;
Luke 23:13-25; John 18:39-40

"Give us Barabbas!"

The prisoner cringed as he heard the mob outside the Roman governor's house. Had his time come so soon? The famous criminal Barabbas was awaiting execution. His crimes: murder, theft, and insurrection. Dragged before the Roman governor Pilate, Barabbas was outwardly defiant but inwardly terrified. The crowd was screaming for blood—his blood. But wait. Barabbas listened again to the shouting crowd. They did not want his blood; they were demanding his freedom!

Another prisoner was present, bound, beaten, and bleeding. He was Jesus the Nazarene who claimed to be the Messiah. Barabbas had heard of this man and His many miracles. Jesus, they said, healed the sick, confounded the wisdom of the scribes and Pharisees, and even raised the dead to life. Yet there He was, tortured and humiliated. Pilate gestured to Jesus and then to Barabbas and asked the bloodthirsty crowd, "Which of these men do you want me to set free?"

Everyone knew that during the yearly Passover celebration Pilate's custom was to release a prisoner of the people's choosing. On this occasion their choice was between the untainted and the terrorist—Jesus and Barabbas. Barabbas could not believe his ears. Not only had the surging crowd chosen him to live, but he would be set free!

Then Pilate washed his hands as a symbol that he was not responsible for taking Jesus' innocent life. It was the crowd (or the crowd's instigators) who were to bear this liability. He ordered Barabbas released and Jesus scourged.

Barabbas said nothing as he waited impatiently for the guards to unshackle him and did not pause to watch the flogging of the Nazarene. Fearful that the people would change their minds, Barabbas fled into the morning, retreated to the back streets of Jerusalem, and disappeared from history.

One may ask, did Barabbas ever wonder about the innocent man who had taken his place on the cross that day—the one who died in his place? Did he repent? Did he believe? Or did the reprieved Barabbas continue to live as a criminal? Does he live today in the understanding of New Testament readers as the model of all of humanity—deserving of death but released to life by the sacrifice of God's Son?

BOAZ
Ruth

Boaz was a wealthy man in Bethlehem during the time of the Old Testament judges. His romance and marriage to the Moabite widow Ruth is a heartwarming story of how God cares for his people in seemingly circuitous ways.

It did not take long for Boaz to notice the young stranger in his field gathering bits of grain left by his reapers. He knew this was Ruth, the foreign woman who had won the admiration of the Israelites because of her steadfast devotion in caring for her mother-in-law Naomi, for whom she was gathering the remnants of grain.

Naomi was a Jewish woman who, with her husband Elimelech and their sons, had been forced out of Bethlehem by famine. They settled in the land of Moab. There Elimelech—who was a relative of Boaz—died as did his two sons. When Naomi determined to return to her native Bethlehem, Ruth, one of her widowed daughters-in-law, vowed to come and care for her. Ruth disagreed with Naomi's reasoning that Ruth would fare better by remaining in her own land. "Wherever you go I will go," said Ruth. "Wherever you live I will live. Your people will be my people and your God will be my God."

And so the two women returned to Bethlehem where Boaz not only allowed Ruth to pick up the leftover grain, he took her under his wing as well. He invited her to eat with him and privately instructed his workers to make sure there was plenty of grain for her to gather.

It occurred to Naomi that Boaz and Ruth would be a likely, godly match. She conspired to make Ruth the focus of Boaz's attention and a mutual interest evolved between Boaz and Ruth.

Then Boaz found a novel way to secure their union. There was one man in Bethlehem who was a closer relative of Elimelech than was Boaz. By law this man had the right to buy from Naomi the land that had belonged to her husband. So Boaz arranged a meeting with the man. Ten elders of the town were present as witnesses.

Boaz proposed that if the man wanted to buy the land he should do so; otherwise, Boaz would buy it.

"Of course I will buy it," the relative replied.

But Boaz pointed out that if the relative acquired the land, he also was obligated to marry Ruth. Their children would inherit the land, and thus the land would legally remain in the family of Ruth's dead husband, Mahlon, Elimelech's son. This the relative could not do, because it would create complications involving other property he owned. Boaz, he decided, could buy the land—and marry Ruth!

So the faithful Ruth and her long-suffering mother-in-law were well provided for. Boaz and Ruth had a son and named him Obed. Obed was the father of Jesse, the father of King David.

CAIN AND ABEL
Genesis 4:1-16; 4:25

Cain was the oldest son of Adam and Eve. Abel was his brother. Cain farmed the soil, Abel was a shepherd. When they brought the Lord offerings of the fruit of their labors, God was not equally impressed. Cain's gift was a sampling of his crops—the Lord did not bless it. The blessing was reserved for the sacrifice of Abel—the choicest meat from his firstborn lamb.

This angered Cain, and the Lord chastised him for being angry and warned, "If you do well, you will be blessed. But if you do wrong, sin will overtake you." Ignoring the warning, Cain killed his brother in a rage.

Later God asked him, "Where is your brother?"

Cain retorted, "Am I my brother's keeper?"

Of course the Lord already knew what had happened and condemned Cain to a life of endless wandering. Never again would the ground he farmed produce food.

"But I'll be homeless," Cain protested, "easy prey for anyone to kill."

So God placed a mark on Cain to warn people not to harm him. But for Cain, death would have been preferable to a roving existence in exile from the presence of God.

DANIEL
Daniel

From the time of his youth, it was obvious Daniel was to be used by the Lord for important work. Then the Babylonians captured Jerusalem. Still, Daniel and three of his friends were outstanding among the Hebrew captives because of their youth, intelligence, handsome appearance, and strength. Therefore they were selected to be trained for service in King Nebuchadnezzar's court.

But Daniel—who had been given the Babylonian name Belteshazzar—demonstrated his determination to live in the godly way in which he had been raised, even if it meant jeopardizing his favored standing among his captors. Nebuchadnezzar ordered that the trainees be given royal food and drink, thinking it would maximize their strength and wit as they grew. But the food was unacceptable according to Jewish custom. Daniel asked his guard to give him and his three friends only vegetables and water.

"What if you end up looking paler than the other trainees?" the guard said.. "Then I'll be killed for disobeying the king's orders."

"Try it for ten days," Daniel suggested. "Then compare us with the other boys."

Not only did they pass the test; their austere, clean diet made them fatter and healthier than the others.

After three years of training, all the young men were interviewed by King Nebuchadnezzar. Daniel and his three friends far surpassed the others in every skill. So the king appointed them to important court positions and relied on their wisdom when he needed advice.

Daniel was particularly wise and had the God-given power to interpret dreams as well. This earned him the king's deepest respect; Daniel was made a governor and named chief counselor. But Daniel made it clear that his abilities did not imply he was in any way superior to any of the other advisors. Rather, he said, God simply had chosen to use him to explain certain things.

Daniel and his friends—whom the Babylonians had named Shadrach, Meshach and Abednego—were faithful to God in the face of their captors' idol worship. On one occasion, Shadrach, Meshach and Abednego were thrown into a furnace for refusing to worship a towering gold statue erected near the city. The heat of the furnace was so intense that it killed the men who guarded it while its intended victims, accompanied by an angel, walked unhurt in the fire. King Nebuchadnezzar was so impressed that he had to respect their God. In time, he himself came to believe in God.

Daniel served under Nebuchadnezzar, his son Belshazzar, King Darius, and later King Cyrus of Persia, and won the highest respect of each of them. It was Belshazzar who commanded that Daniel interpret the mysterious handwriting that appeared on the wall of the king's banquet hall. The message, Daniel accurately interpreted, foretold the end of Belshazzar's reign.

During Darius's reign, governors and officials who were jealous of Daniel's wisdom and power contrived to have the king issue a decree forbidding anyone in the kingdom to pray to any god—on pain of death! Naturally Daniel continued to pray daily. This was reported to Darius. He was horrified because to uphold his decree he would have to order the execution of Daniel, his most trusted advisor. Reluctantly he had Daniel cast into a den of lions and then prayed himself that God would save his servant.

And God did so by sending an angel to keep the lions at bay throughout the night. In the morning Darius ordered Daniel released and his accusers thrown to the lions. Then the king ordered everyone in his kingdom to worship Daniel's God whom Darius recognized as the one true God.

DAVID
1 Samuel 16:1–1 Kings 2:11

David was the greatest of Israel's kings. His forty-year reign was a rollercoaster of amazing gains and foolish losses, exemplary leadership and shocking failure. Yet he was a man after God's own heart.

The great prophet Samuel was dispatched to the house of Jesse in Bethlehem. One of Jesse's sons was to succeed Saul as king of Israel. One by one Jesse paraded his seven older sons before Samuel. But God told Samuel to reject each of them. Finally Jesse called for his youngest son David, a hardy, sunburned shepherd. "Anoint him," God told Samuel and God's Spirit came upon David—and left King Saul. David soon entered Saul's service as a musician, playing his harp to soothe the king's troubled mind.

David's most famous act occurred at this time. The Philistine army was gathered to fight the Israelites near Shochoh. Each day Goliath, the giant soldier of the Philistines, strutted from the Philistine camp and taunted the Israelites camped across the valley. He challenged the bravest of them to come out and fight him. The Jewish soldiers, including David's own brothers, knew the giant could not be beaten, so they cowered in disgrace.

One day David arrived in camp with food for his brothers. "Who is this uncircumcised enemy who defies the army of the Lord?" he demanded and immediately asked Saul for permission to take on the giant. Under-standably, Saul refused because of David's youth, modest size, and inexperience. But David pointed out that as a shepherd he had killed a lion and bear when they had raided his flock. And in any case, David knew the Lord would protect him. The king assented.

Declining Saul's heavy sword and armor, David selected a few smooth stones from a brook and, sling in hand, approached the haughty giant. Goliath, angry that the Israelites had sent a boy with no sword or armor to fight him, cursed the youth. "I will feed your flesh to the animals," he snarled.

David replied, "You come to me with heavy weapons, but I come to you in God's name. Today I'm going to take your head, and your army will be defeated, for this is the Lord's battle."

And so it happened. One stone hurled from David's sling was all it took. Struck solidly in the forehead, Goliath fell on his face, killed instantly. David chopped off Goliath's head with the giant's own sword, and the Israelites attacked and routed the demoralized Philistines.

For the rest of his life—while fleeing from jealous Saul to the years of his own kingship—David sought the Lord's will. His love and reverence for God live today in many of the psalms he penned. But other psalms speak from deepest human despair, for David frequently was tested. He also made serious mistakes. His lust for Bathsheba, for example, led him not only to adultery but to conspire to commit murder.

He also was one of the most incompetent parents in Scripture. He loved his sons passionately, but could not bring himself to discipline them. Tragedy upon tragedy resulted, first with Amnon, then with Absalom and Adonijah.

David designated his son Solomon to succeed him as king and instructed him just before death. This advice elucidates David's character: "Obey the Lord your God. Walk in his ways, and keep his laws."

ELIJAH
1 Kings 17:1-2 Kings 2:11

Prophesies are not always ominous or kingdom-shat-tering. In the instance of Elijah and the widow of Zarephath, the issue was providing food for a family.

Elijah met the woman at the city gate after obeying God's command to journey to Zarephath. There he requested of her water and bread. She responded that she was so poor that she had only a little flour and oil; she was planning to use the last of it to prepare a meal for herself and her son. After this she fully expected to starve to death. Elijah told her to prepare the meal as planned—but first to make him a little bread. When she did that he told her, "The Lord will see to it that your flour bin and oil jar remain full."

And, to the woman's amazement, this happened. A short time later her son became ill and died. In her anguish she questioned the fairness of Elijah and his God. So Elijah took the child upstairs and prayed for the child to be brought back to life. He stretched his body over the corpse and God warmed the body and breathed life back into the boy. The woman could no longer doubt. "Now," she said, "I know you are a godly man and the Lord has given you His truth to preach."

Other issues for this prophet from Gilead were significant on a national level. Elijah was a contemporary of King Ahab and wicked Queen Jezebel of the northern kingdom of Israel. Under Ahab, the people worshipped Baal instead of God.

Elijah, who in Ahab's words was the "troubler of Israel," challenged the king and his Baal-worshipping prophets to a contest on Mount Carmel. Crowds of Israelites stood by as witnesses. He proposed that two bulls be sacrificed by fire. Ahab's prophets would summon Baal to light the fire beneath their sacrifice, then Elijah would call on the name of the Lord to ignite his offering.

Elijah had great fun mocking the futile, frantic, protracted attempts of the heathen prophets to get Baal to do something—anything at all. "Perhaps Baal is busy with other things," Elijah taunted, "or away on a trip. Maybe he's asleep and doesn't want to be bothered." All day long they tried to cajole Baal into lighting the fire. Of course, nothing happened. Finally they gave up.

When it was his turn, Elijah set up God's miracle with a flourish. He built an altar with twelve stones, symbolic of the twelve tribes of Israel. He dug a trench around it, laid on the wood, and put the meat of the bull on the wood. Then he ordered everything thoroughly drenched with water, making it seemingly impossible for a fire to burn. The trench surrounding the altar was filled with water. Elijah then prayed to God to turn the people's hearts back to Him.

God not only lit the wet altar but made the fire so intense it dried up the surrounding trench. The people were quite convinced. They rounded up the heathen prophets, and Elijah executed them.

When Queen Jezebel heard the news, she vowed to kill Elijah and the remainder of the prophet's life was spent in tension and confrontation with Ahab and Jezebel, and their successor Ahaziah. Elijah performed dramatic miracles which affirmed God's power and glory.

And Elijah did not die. Instead, as he was walking with the prophet Elisha, a chariot of fire appeared and Elijah was carried upward in a whirlwind. Centuries later the apostles Peter, James, and John saw Elijah appear with Jesus at the Transfiguration, and the Bible tells us Elijah himself will return before the final judgment. Clearly, Elijah was a prophet of unique importance with a role to play in God's kingdom far beyond his earthly generation.

ELISHA
1 Kings 19:15-21; 2 Kings 2:1-8:15; 13:14-21

God chose Elisha to succeed Elijah as chief prophet in the ninth century B.C. Elisha was with Elijah when the great prophet was carried heavenward in the whirlwind. Then Elisha picked up the cloak Elijah left behind and went to the nearby Jordan River. Was the Lord empowering him to be the next prophet? When Elijah struck the water with the cloak, God opened a path for him to cross the river and confirmed his prophethood.

Elisha performed many miracles including the provision of an inexplicably boundless supply of oil that paid a widow's debts; the prophecy of a son for a childless woman in Shunem who indeed bore a son. But the boy died and Elisha brought him back to life.

Another of Elisha's miracles was his feeding of a hundred men with a few loaves of bread, much like the Lord Jesus would feed the multitudes in a later era. Also like Jesus, Elisha healed the leper Naaman. And his uncanny knowledge repeatedly foiled the warring Arameans' attacks against Israel. Elisha always performed his miracles and prophecies to draw attention not to himself, but to God.

God honored this devotion, even beyond Elisha's death. An astonishing postscript to his story is recorded in 2 Kings 13:20-21. Sometime after the prophet's burial some Israelites were in the process of another burial when they were interrupted by a band of Moabites. In their haste to escape the raiders, the burial party flung the corpse into Elisha's tomb. When the body touched the bones of the dead prophet, it came back to life!

The story of this prophet/patriarch lives on to remind us that God can and does use dedicated believers as agents of his incredible power and goodness.

ESAU

Genesis 25:21-34; 26:34-35;
27:1-28:9; 32:3-21; 33:1-16; 36:1-19

Esau and Jacob were twin brothers, sons of Isaac and Rebekah. Their relationship was not a peaceful one. Even inside their mother's womb they clashed. "Two nations are inside your womb," God explained to Rebekah. "One will be stronger, and the oldest will serve the youngest." Esau was delivered first, with Jacob following behind clutching his brother's heel. And, as God had said, Esau was left out of the Hebrew lineage despite his birthright as the firstborn son.

It happened this way: Isaac came to favor Esau as the boy grew because Esau was an excellent hunter and brought his father wild game to eat. Jacob, more inclined toward domestic life, became Rebekah's favorite. One day Esau came home from the wilds extremely hungry and asked for some of the stew Jacob was cooking. "Trade me your birthright for it," Jacob said. Famished, Esau unthinkingly swore to give Jacob his birthright.

Some time later this verbal theft of Esau's birthright came into effect when Rebekah and Jacob tricked Isaac, who was old and blind, into granting his blessing to Jacob. Isaac had sent Esau into the wild to kill an animal and prepare the meat in Isaac's favorite way. Isaac promised that after he ate the wild game he would bless Esau. Rebekah overheard Isaac's words and told Jacob to kill some goats nearby. She used them to prepare the special meal and sent

Jacob into Isaac's tent dressed in Esau's clothes so he would smell and feel like Esau. Isaac would never know the difference. Jacob served his father the meal and received the blessing of the firstborn son in place of Esau.

The ruse worked. Jacob received the blessing that by right should have been given to Esau, the true firstborn. Part of the blessing was the headship of the family. "May all who curse you be cursed, and all who bless you be blessed," Isaac said.

Shortly afterward Esau returned with the game, prepared it the way his father liked, and took it to Isaac hoping to receive his blessing. But Isaac could not revoke the blessing he had already given Jacob even though he had made a mistake. So Esau was designated to serve his younger brother just as God had foretold. Esau was furious and vowed to kill Jacob as soon as their father died. So Jacob fled to Haran to live with their uncle Laban.

Many years later, Jacob sought to reconcile with Esau. Imagine Jacob's fear when Esau came to meet him with an army of several hundred men! Jacob sent a generous offering of livestock to Esau. As they approached each other, Jacob bowed low seven times to pay homage to his brother. Esau forgot his wrath and tearfully ran to embrace and forgive Jacob for his deception.

Pardon can rarely be as moving as when Esau reconciled with the brother who had stolen his birthright.

EZEKIEL
Ezekiel

D em bones, dem bones, dem dry bones. . .

Dem bones gonna rise again. . . .

Apart from the African-American spirituals we have sung for generations, most Christians have only a sketchy acquaintance with the prophet Ezekiel.

Ezekiel prophesied in the sixth century B.C. just before Jerusalem's fall and as the Jews were exiled into Babylon. He had a singular encounter with the Lord who showed him an astounding vision: Four living creatures, each with four faces, and four wings, appeared within a shining windstorm; each creature had four faces, one of a human, a lion, a bull, and an eagle; beside each creature was a bright wheel within a wheel with eyes around the rims. At length Ezekiel realized he was witnessing a form of the Lord's glory. In this way God appointed Ezekiel to prophesy to the Israelites.

Early in his book Ezekiel warned the people of Judah that their sins would bring about the ruination of Jerusalem. He predicted the captivity of the Jews and urged the people to return to the Lord's ways. Ultimately he described Jerusalem as a worthless vine that needed to be punished and put to shame. He also predicted God's judgment against rival nations: Ammon, Moab, Edom, Philistia, Tyre, and Egypt.

A most memorable part of Ezekiel's prophecy is his vision of the nation of Israel as dry bones laying in a valley. God promised that He would free these dead, hope-less bones from their entombment and cause them to live again.

Ezekiel foretold the restoration of Jerusalem and de-scribed in detail how the temple would be rebuilt. He explained the way worship would be conducted in that new temple and how the land would be subdivided among the Israelites upon their return. His prophecy covers the concerns of the captive people with warnings, encourage-ment, and assurances that they would in time regain their lost kingdom.

EZRA AND NEHEMIAH
Ezra 7:1-10:17; Nehemiah

Ezra and Nehemiah emerged during a pivotal time in Jewish history. After decades of captivity in Babylon, they led many people back to Judah to rebuild Jerusalem and her temple both structurally and spiritually.

Ezra, a priest and scholar versed in God's law, was a descendant of Aaron, the first high priest. He was in charge of some of the returning exiles. A wonderfully devout man, Ezra led his flock in prayer and fasting. His role was to end the practice of Jews marrying non-Jews from neighboring countries and to return the people to God's ordained pat-tern of worship.

Meanwhile Nehemiah was still living in Persia where he served as the emperor's wine steward. Nehemiah learned of the difficulties the Jews were encountering in Jerusalem. They lived in fear of surrounding nations, and the protective wall around Jerusalem was in ruins. The Persian emperor granted him permission to go to Jerusalem and supervise the rebuilding of the city's wall. In fact, God so stirred the emperor's heart that Nehemiah was given an escort and building materials.

As the Israelites worked on the wall, their enemies plotted against them. God repeatedly thwarted these plots. Nehemiah prayed often and calmed his people's fears by organizing the workers: Half of them, fully armed, stood guard while the other half toiled at the wall. Even the wall builders carried swords.

When the wall was finished it was obvious to both the Israelites and their enemies that God's hand had been upon its building. The people asked Ezra to read the law to them, then they prayed, confessed their sins and the sins of their ancestors, and signed an agreement to live in obedience to God.

God's work is often fraught with danger and uncertainty. During the period of the restoration of Jerusalem the Israelites could not rest easy. Their leaders had to be alert and live in close contact with God. Ezra and Nehemiah rose to this demand.

GIDEON
Judges 6-8

He was not a man to be trifled with, as many a foe discovered. Happily, Gideon was on the side of the Israelites.

During the time of the judges God let Israel be subjugated by Midian, and for seven years the children of Israel were impoverished victims of their conquerors.

After they had suffered long enough the Lord spoke to Gideon. This poor Israelite from Ophrah was trying to horde a supply of wheat from his captors, but God had more important work for him to do. God told Gideon, "You will save Israel from the hand of the Midianites."

Gideon was afraid—not only of the assignment, but of his encounter with God. His tribe was weak, Gideon protested, and he was the lowest member of his own family. The Lord responded by bringing the Spirit upon Gideon.

Thus empowered, Gideon sounded a trumpet and sent messengers to gather an army. Thirty-two thousand men initially joined him. "This is too many," God told him. If Israel won the victory with such a large army the people would assume credit for themselves and deny the power of God. So Gideon invited those who were afraid of fighting to turn back. This left him with ten thousand soldiers.

"Still too many," the Lord said—doubtless stirring Gideon's uneasiness. To reduce the number of soldiers further, God told Gideon to send the soldiers to the water's edge and drink. The ones who lapped the water as a dog would drink were to be separated from those who knelt to drink the water cupped in their hands. Three hundred men lapped to drink. God told Gideon to discharge all the others. "I will deliver the Midianites into your hands."

The Midianites camped in the valley were as thick as locusts; their camels were as numerous as sand on the seashore. Gideon naturally was timid so the Lord told him to slip into the Midianite camp at night and promised to show him a sign there for reassurance. When Gideon crept near the Midianite camp he heard two men talking. One was relating a dream he'd had of a bread loaf tumbling into camp and flattening one of the tents. His friend interpreted the dream: "The bread loaf is the sword of the Israelite, Gideon. God will deliver the whole Midianite camp into his hands!" Gideon knew his mission was secure.

Gideon and his men took trumpets, jars, and torches and surrounded the Midianite camp. When signaled they sounded the horns, smashed the jars, and waved the torches. The sudden clamor on all sides wakened the Midianites to a scene of total confusion. In their rush to escape they mistakenly attacked and killed many of their own comrades.

Other Israelites were summoned and completely routed the Midianites. As Gideon and his three hundred commandos chased the Midianite kings across the Jordan River, they wearily stopped at the towns of Succoth and Penuel and requested food, but the leaders of both towns refused to help them. Gideon angrily warned that when he returned with the two kings in tow the insolent town leaders would be punished severely. He was as good as his word. Succoth and Penuel were punished and the captured kings of Midian were put to death.

The grateful Israelites wanted Gideon and his descendants to be their rulers. But Gideon responded, "The Lord will rule over you."

Gideon's story ends on the unhappy note of forgetfulness and idolatry. In the aftermath of his unprecedented victory Gideon collected the gold earrings captured from the Midianites. They were melted and cast into an idol which Gideon took to his hometown of Ophrah. Then, as is the pattern in the book of Judges, Israel forgot God and gathered in Ophrah to worship Gideon's idol.

HEROD ANTIPAS
Matthew 14:1-12; Mark 6:14-29; Luke 23:7-12

Unscrupulous yet cautious, Herod Antipas ruled Galilee during the lifetime of Jesus Christ. His father, Herod the Great, had been completely heartless when he ordered the cold-blooded killing of every baby boy around Bethlehem in an attempt to eliminate the newborn king of the Jews. Like his father, the younger Herod had no love for Jesus or for John the Baptist. Their ministries were causing an unprecedented sensation throughout the land but Herod Antipas was not as ruthless as his father. In fact he tried to avoid the conflict which these men would cause him.

Yet Herod Antipas had a particular disdain for John. Herod had taken his brother Philip's wife as his own and

John had boldly pointed out his wrongdoing. The king wanted to arrest and execute John for this, but he was afraid the people would revolt because of their high regard for John.

Then the wife in question, Herodias, forced Herod's hand. She persuaded Herod to have John arrested. Then, using her daughter's sensuous dancing to corrupt his thinking, Herodias obtained an order to have John beheaded. This unnerved the ruler. Not only did he fear the people's reaction, he privately appreciated John's preaching. But he had promised to do whatever his pretty niece wanted, and, at her mother's request, she asked that John be beheaded and his head presented to her on a platter. So it was done.

When Jesus Christ was arrested and dragged before Pilate in Jerusalem, Herod happened to be in the city. Pilate tried to take advantage of this in an effort to shift the role of judge to Herod Antipas. So Pilate sent Jesus and His accusers to Herod. After all, Jesus was a Galilean, so His case came under Herod's authority. Herod was eager to meet Jesus because he wanted to see Him perform a miracle. But Jesus refused to answer Herod's questions. So Herod and his soldiers mocked the prisoner and sent Him back to Pilate.

Scripture says Herod and Pilate, who had been enemies, became friends in the aftermath of Jesus' crucifixion. These two cowardly leaders found a common bond at the turning point of civilization. They may have feared this man from Galilee, but they could not acknowledge the existence of a power above their own or that of Rome.

HEZEKIAH
2 Kings 18:1-20:21

The Old Testament grimly testifies that Israel had its share of bad rulers. A refreshing exception was Hezekiah. His reign began around 710 B.C. when he was twenty-five years old. Hezekiah "did that which was right in the sight of the Lord." He was completely faithful. No other king before or after him was his peer in this regard. In return the Lord blessed him and helped him prevail against the enemies of Israel.

Hezekiah's greatest challenge came early in his reign when Assyria invaded Judah. "Don't listen to Hezekiah," the Assyrian commander told the frightened Israelites. "His God won't protect you. No other kingdoms have been able to withstand our might. Surrender to us, and live in peace." The Jews began to believe him and to doubt the wisdom and ability of their devout leader.

Hezekiah turned to the great prophet Isaiah for counsel, and Isaiah reassured him that the Lord had doomed the Assyrian invasion to confusion and failure. So it proved. King Sennacherib of Assyria returned to Nineveh and ultimately was murdered by his own sons.

King Hezekiah became deathly ill to the point that even Isaiah predicted he would die. But Hezekiah prayed; the Lord heard, and sent Isaiah to announce that the king would live another fifteen years.

Though godly and faithful, Hezekiah did not always make wise decisions. While Hezekiah was sick, the king of

Babylonia sent messengers bearing a gift. Gratified by this display of kindness Hezekiah gave the Babylonian envoys a detailed tour of his country's storehouses and armaments. In fact there was no strategic secret in all of Judah that Hezekiah didn't imprudently reveal to these seemingly friendly visitors. God told Hezekiah through Isaiah that the result of his carelessness would be the Babylonian conquest of Judah. This occurred a century later.

Hezekiah ruled for twenty-nine years. He was succeeded by his twelve-year-old son Manasseh, who shunned his father's righteous ways and returned to the idol worship Hezekiah had denounced.

HOSEA
Hosea

The unfaithful wife deserted her husband for a lover. The husband paid her return to his household! This, the story of the prophet Hosea, parallels the message he brought to the people of Israel. Israel had betrayed their Lord like a promiscuous wife, yet God in His mercy was willing to buy them back!

Hosea could understand the agonizing relationship between God and His wayward people better than any other prophet because he knew similar agony in his own life. He could speak to the Israelites bluntly and harshly but with genuine underlying love. He knew of the pain they were causing their Maker by their long history of disobedience.

And God's pain was heightened by the fact that He loved them passionately.

Hosea's prophecy contained a straightforward accusation against the people's sins and idolatry. "Judgment is coming," he warned. "Bondage will follow. You have trusted in your own power so you will reap destruction."

But near the end of his book Hosea poignantly conveyed God's irrevocable love for His people. "How can I give you up?" God said. "I am not man, I am God and I love you tenderly. I will not vent My wrath on you." Hosea concludes with a plea that Israel repent, and a final assurance of God's forgiveness if the people would only turn back to Him.

ISAAC
Genesis 18:10-15; 21:1-13;
22:1-18; 24:1-67; 25:19-28:5; 35:27-29

Laughter was the meaning of his name because his birth brought great rejoicing. He was God's promise to his aged parents Abraham and Sarah.

Isaac's upbringing was stamped with a unique demonstration of love and obedience to God. His trek into the land of Moriah with Abraham, the building of the altar in the middle of nowhere, the binding of his hands and feet, his placement on the altar, his father's upraised knife—then, in that moment of incredible terror, when the child could neither understand nor believe what was being done to him, came the saving cry of God's angel—"Abraham!

Abraham!"

The knife was stayed. "Now I know," the angel told Abraham, "that you love God above all else—even more than your son who is so precious to you."

Isaac's is the earliest love story. Abraham did not want Isaac to marry any of the women in Canaan. He instructed his chief servant to travel east to Abraham's homeland and find a wife for Isaac. "God will send His angel before you," Abraham assured the servant.

The servant took ten camels and many gifts and departed. Outside the city of Haran, he stopped at a spring. This was the end of the day and the women of the city were coming out to draw water. The servant prayed that God would show him the woman who was to be Isaac's wife. This would be the test: The servant would ask for a drink of water; the woman, if she was the right one, would offer water not only to him but to his camels.

Immediately a beautiful young woman named Rebekah, granddaughter of Abraham's brother Nahor, came to the spring. "Please let me have some water from your jar," the servant said.

"Drink," she said, lowering her jar. Then she drew more water for the camels.

Invited to stay the night with Rebekah's family, the servant told them the story of his mission and of the test at the spring. "It is God's will," agreed Rebekah's father. He asked Rebekah if she would go with the envoy and become Isaac's wife. "I will," she said.

One evening Isaac was walking in the field when he saw the servant returning. With the servant was a young woman who had her face veiled. Isaac married Rebekah and, since this was not long after his mother Sarah's death, was comforted in his grief. He loved Rebekah very dearly.

The couple were blessed by God. Isaac became very wealthy. But their twin sons Esau and Jacob were to open a stormy chapter in the history of God's people. The details of their dramatic rivalry are recounted separately in this book. Thankfully, by the time of Isaac's death in Hebron at age 180, Esau and Jacob had reconciled.

ISAIAH
Isaiah

Isaiah is one of the best-known Hebrew prophets. He spoke for God in Jerusalem during the eighth century B.C. at the time when Assyria conquered Israel and carried many victims into exile.

According to Isaiah's own description, he was a Jew "of unclean lips" living in an unclean nation. In a vision he saw the Lord sitting on a throne attended by winged seraphs. One of the seraphs took a live coal from the Lord's altar, flew down, and touched Isaiah's lips with the coal. "Now your record has been blotted clean, and you no longer are guilty," the angel told him.

The Lord needed a spokesman to show the Israelites their sins and turn them back to His ways. "Whom shall I send?" God asked.

"Here I am," responded the awestruck Isaiah. "Send me."

Isaiah prophesied for forty years during the reigns of four kings. He knew the Israelites had much more to fear from their own wrongdoing and lack of faith than they did from the Assyrians. He preached to Israel before and after their captivity. He reminded them of God's faithfulness to their ancestors and taught them that God is in control of all history.

"Do you think I have divorced you like a man divorces his wife?" God asked the downtrodden Israelites through His prophet. "Then where are the divorce papers?" God still loved His people, Isaiah proclaimed, and would rescue them. He said that the Lord was building a new creation, a place of peace, where there would be no sorrow or death. "Therefore rejoice!" Isaiah exhorted.

Throughout his prophecies Isaiah foretells the coming of the Messiah, a descendant of Jesse, a cornerstone, shepherd, and bearer of salvation. With good reason Isaiah cried, "Rejoice!"

ISHMAEL
Genesis 16; 21:9-21

Ishmael was the son of scheming and jealousy.

Abraham and Sarah were childless. Sarah, frustrated by her barren condition, formulated a solution. She gave Abraham her Egyptian maid Hagar as his wife, so Hagar could bear a child on Sarah's behalf. After she became pregnant, Hagar could not hide her feelings of contempt toward her barren mistress, Sarah. Angrily Sarah mistreated her and Hagar fled into the wilderness. An angel found her there deeply distressed and admonished her to return to Sarah's service. The angel told her that her newborn son should be called Ishmael, that he would be a wild man, and contend with many people. Yet Ishmael would give Hagar a line of descendants too numerous to count.

So Hagar returned with Ishmael to the house of Abraham and Sarah.

Ishmael was a teenager when God finally gave a son to Abraham and Sarah. With the birth of Isaac, tension mounted within the household. Sarah wanted to make sure their entire inheritance went to her son Isaac, so she demanded that Abraham send Hagar and Ishmael away.

Abraham did not want to do this. He was afraid Hagar and Ishmael would not survive. But the Lord assured him, "Your son Isaac will have your inheritance and continue your lineage, but your son Ishmael also will father a great nation."

Abraham sent the servant woman and her son away with water and bread. Roaming through the wilderness near Beersheba, they soon ran out of food and water. Hagar placed her son in the shade of a bush then stumbled off so she would not have to see him die.

In the depth of her despair, Hagar was again visited by an angel who led her to a well of water. "Do not worry," the angel said, "Ishmael will survive and become the father of a long line of descendants."

Ishmael grew up to be a great hunter and his mother found an Egyptian woman for him to marry. He did not receive his father's inheritance but Ishmael nevertheless was richly blessed as the Lord had promised his mother.

JACOB
Genesis 25:19-49:33

Jacob came into the world clutching his twin brother's heel. This was symbolic of struggles to come. Jacob contended with his older brother Esau over the birthright and the blessing of their father Isaac. Jacob won, but only through deception. The story of the enmity and eventual reconciliation of these patriarchs is told earlier in this book in the account of Esau.

After stealing the blessing from Esau, Jacob fled to northern Syria to live with his uncle Laban. During the journey he stopped one night to sleep and used a rock for a pillow. There Jacob had a dream of a ladder that reached from earth to heaven. Angels were climbing up and down on this ladder. In the dream the Lord promised Jacob that his descendants would cover the earth and that He would be with Jacob in his travels.

When he awoke Jacob was frightened and said, "This is the house of God and the gate of heaven!" He named the place Bethel and promised that if God would take care of him, he would always worship God and return to the Lord a tenth of everything he ever received.

Welcomed into his uncle Laban's household, Jacob fell in love with Laban's daughter Rachel. He told Laban he would work for him seven years if Laban would give him Rachel's hand in marriage. Laban agreed.

The seven years flew by, or so it seemed to Jacob. He was head over heels in love with Rachel. When Laban arranged the wedding he gave his older daughter Leah to be Jacob's wife instead of Rachel. Jacob furiously protested. Laban explained the custom—the oldest daughter marries first! He promised to let Jacob marry Rachel too, but only if Jacob would work another seven years! Jacob agreed and eventually had both daughters as wives. But he always preferred Rachel.

God saw that Leah was unloved and allowed her to have children while Rachel was unable to conceive. Jacob had six sons by Leah, two other sons by Leah's maid, and two sons by Rachel's maid. Finally God remembered Rachel and let her have a son of her own; his name was Joseph. Later Rachel died giving birth to her second son—Jacob's twelfth—who was called Benjamin.

In time, relations between Jacob and Laban became very strained. Laban was not happy that Jacob's livestock multiplied and grew healthier than the other herds. Jacob yearned to return with his household to his homeland, but Laban realized that the Lord's blessings on Jacob over the years had had a positive effect on his own fortunes. Ultimately Jacob and his family fled in secret. Laban and his men chased and caught them, but conflict was averted and Jacob and Laban made a pact and parted peacefully.

During the journey back to his homeland, Jacob wrestled with God who appeared in the form of a man. All night they wrestled and Jacob's hip was thrown out of joint in the struggle but he was not defeated. As daylight approached and the man began to leave, Jacob refused to let Him go until he received a blessing from the divine opponent.

"From now on," the man said, "your name will be Israel, because you have wrestled with God and with men and have won."

JAMES THE BROTHER OF JESUS
Matthew 13:55; Mark 6:3;
Acts 12:17; 15:12-21; 21:18; Gal. 1:19

Imagine growing up the brother of Jesus Christ and not knowing that He was the promised Messiah until after the Crucifixion and Ascension.

James knew how Jesus liked His eggs cooked; how He reacted after hitting His thumb with a hammer; how He handled incidents of sibling banter and rivalry; His favorite games. As James grew up with Jesus he did not know that his brother was the incarnate God. Years later he surely remembered the incidents of Jesus' childhood, adolescence, and young manhood with a different understanding.

Some scholars think that James did not become a believer until after Jesus' death and resurrection. Details of his life are few and learning about him is difficult because the New Testament records four men by the name of James. After Jesus' resurrection, was it his brother James who became head of the first century church in Jerusalem? Was he the writer of the New Testament letter bearing his name? Some scholars suspect so; others are not sure.

Regardless, envision yourself as Jesus' own brother!

JEREMIAH
Jeremiah

If you think you're too young or too ordinary to be used by God, consider Jeremiah. He was probably still in his teens when God called him to prophesy in Judah. Jeremiah thought he was too young and not a particularly good speaker. But the Lord would have none of these protests. "Go where I tell you to go," God commanded. "Do not be afraid; I'll be with you." He touched Jeremiah's mouth and told him, "I have put My words in your mouth."

The Lord sent Jeremiah to Jerusalem where the prophet delivered God's indictment to the sinful, idolatrous people. He pointed out their unfaithfulness and that of their ancestors. He asked them to return to God. He repeatedly warned of invasion from the north: Jerusalem was about to be devastated. Jeremiah went so far as to tell the Israelites to surrender to the Babylonians rather than die in battle.

The people were not happy to hear this message, especially coming from one so young. But Jeremiah also preached that the Lord would rescue the Israelites and rebuild their nation after they returned to Him. But that did not mollify the people's anger. The Jews plotted to kill Jeremiah and actually threw him in prison for his preaching.

More than any other prophet, Jeremiah revealed his own

disgruntlement and questions. "You told us we would have peace, but a sword is at our throats," he whined to God. He personally agonized as he told the people of their coming defeat. When they laughed at him, he expressed his anger openly.

Perhaps because of his youth, Jeremiah held nothing back. But he was mature spiritually. This is seen in his prayer, "I know we humans are not in control. Punish me as I deserve—but not in anger, for that would kill me." Jeremiah reminds us that God is in control of every situation.

JESUS CHRIST

For the prophets He is the Messiah.
    For Mary He is a son.
For God He is the Son.
    For Herod He is a threat.
For the wise men He is King of the Jews.
    For the shepherds He is heralded by angels.
For Simeon He is the consolation of Israel.
    For the religious leaders He is a challenger.
For His fellow Nazarenes He is an outcast.
    For the demon-possessed He is the liberator.
For the blind He is the giver of sight.
    For the lame He is the transformer.
For the dead He is the reviver.
    For the hungry multitude He is the provider.
For children He is the defender.

For sinners He is forgiveness.
For the ignorant He is the teacher.
For the storm-tossed He walks on water.
For the diseased He is the healer.
For lost sheep He is the shepherd.
For the sins of the world He is the Lamb of God.
For Thomas He is an enigma.
For Judas Iscariot He is a profit source.
For Pontius Pilate He is an annoyance.
For witnesses of the Crucifixion He is contemptuous.
And for all who receive Him, who believe in His name,
He gives power to become children of God.

How could the people of the first century believe that the Messiah had at long last arrived? Jesus Christ was certainly not what they expected. He did not act like a king, or even a priest. He selected commoners, even sinners, for companions and loved the poor, the rich, the young, the old, the Jew, the Gentile, the persecutor, and the persecuted. There was no one He did not love.

There is no one Jesus Christ does not love. He receives all who come to Him and can be reached instantly by anyone from anywhere. One can never intrude upon Jesus. He waits to hear from you!

JOAB

2 Samuel 2:8-3:39; 8:15-18; 10:1-14; 11:1-25;
12:26-27; 14:1-33; 18:1-19:7; 20:6-23;
1 Kings 1:1-2:35;
1 Chronicles 11:6-8; 19:8-15; 20:1; 21:1-7

Civil war was brewing. King Saul was dead and the people of Judah wanted David to be their king. Meanwhile to the north in Israel, the army commander Abner had made Saul's son Ish-bosheth a puppet king; Abner himself held the real power. Men who once respected each other had become enemies.

Joab and his brothers Abishai and Asahel were warriors for David. But Abner killed Joab's brother Asahel, and Joab was angered when Abner made a pact with David. Without David's knowledge, Joab arranged a meeting with Abner and murdered him in cold blood. Dismayed, David ordered his people to mourn for Abner and prayed that God would punish Joab and his family.

This set the tone of David and Joab's relationship. When David became king of all Israel, Joab was the commander of his army. Joab proved to be a clever, brave military leader who always wanted to do what he thought was best for David. But he sometimes did things his own way and was never afraid to speak his mind to the king. For example, David's rebellious son Absalom tried to take over the kingship. A battle ensued and David wanted his soldiers to let Absalom live. But Joab knew David's softheartedness would only result in future trouble with Absalom. So, while Absalom hung by his hair, helpless in a tree, Joab killed him.

At the end of David's reign, Joab allied himself with David's son Adonijah who wanted to take over the throne. David instead chose his son Solomon to succeed him. On his deathbed David cited Joab's disrespect to Solomon. "Punish him as you will," David said. "Do not let him die in peace."

Solomon wasted little time securing his position as king. He dispatched Benaiah, who had been the captain of David's bodyguard and would become Solomon's army commander, to kill Adonijah and Joab. And so, this clever player in the game of politics and war ultimately was paid in violence for his choices.

JOB
Job

"Y ou have the patience of Job."

Smile if someone pays you that compliment because Job was one of the most honorable characters in the Bible. He was a wealthy man whose family, fortune, health, and friendships were suddenly taken from him for no apparent reason. Yet he refused to succumb to unbelief. Though he languished aloud, Job knew his Lord had a reason for his predicament and he patiently waited for things to be made right.

Job lived in the land of Uz and was a faithful believer in

God. In fact, God told Satan that Job was the most faithful man in the world.

"The only reason he worships You," Satan retorted, "is that You protect him and bless everything he does. How do You think he would behave if You let him lose all he has? He'll curse You."

"We'll see," God said and let Job's wonderful world collapse around him.

Afterwards Job was visited by three friends, Eliphaz, Bildad, and Zophar. They came to comfort him, but they were hardly a comfort to this godly man. They did not understand Job's devout faith. It seemed apparent to them that Job was being punished because he had done something wrong.

Job knew better. He was not perfect, but he certainly had not committed enough sins to warrant the intensity of sufferings he had been given. Although he demanded to know why God had let him fall into such a state and even became very angry with God, Job never lost faith.

God's reply was a stern and eloquent reminder of His incredible power and the insignificance of human understanding. Job apologized for questioning the Lord's decisions. Then God turned His reproach on the three friends for misinterpreting the meaning of Job's plight. In the end, God made Job twice as wealthy as before.

When we see good people around us afflicted with terrible diseases, tragedies, and setbacks, we should remember Job who lost everything but his understanding of God's faithfulness.

JOEL
Joel

Locusts!

The plague that swept through Israel around the fifth century B.C. was one of the most dramatic in Old Testament history. God used it to punish His sinful people and through the prophet Joel promised His forgiveness if they changed their ways.

Joel likened the locusts to a hostile army, a nation, and "a people great and strong." Far too many to be counted, the locusts were laying waste the land of Israel which once had been as fruitful as the Garden of Eden. These locusts got Israel's attention and then Joel sounded the alarm. Hopefully the Israelites would listen to his warning of judgment day.

Joel prophesied that when Israel repented God would bless them again by sending His Holy Spirit. Their descendants would be prophets and visionaries. Their enemies would be punished and the faithful would be saved. He spoke of the day of judgment when the sun would be darkened, the moon turned to blood, and enemy nations would lie desolate. But God's people would find refuge in a land where the mountains "drop down with sweet wine" and the hills "flow with milk."

Joel's is a prophecy of stark contrasts—light and darkness, good and evil, struggles in punishment and rest in God's presence.

JOHN THE APOSTLE
Matthew 4:21-22;
Mark 1:9-20; 10:35-45;
the Gospel of John; Acts 3:1-4:31; 8:14-17;
1, 2 and 3 John; Revelation

John and his brother James followed in the footsteps of their father Zebedee and became fishermen. Their friends, the brothers Andrew and Peter, were also fishermen. All four were called to be His disciples by Christ early in His ministry.

In his gospel, John gave us firsthand accounts of many of the Savior's miracles, beginning with the wedding at Cana where Jesus turned the water into wine, all the way to Jesus' visitations after His resurrection. Although John did not record all the miracles he saw, he offered ample proof that Jesus is the Son of God.

John's gospel makes effective use of metaphor: In it Jesus is a Shepherd to His flock, the Living Bread and the Water of Life, the Light of the World, and the True Vine. John was a brilliant thinker, an eloquent writer, and passionate in his devotion to the Savior. So much so that from the cross Jesus asked him to care for His mother.

After Jesus' ascension, John labored among the churches in Asia Minor and is credited with writing Revelation and the epistles of John. Historians believe that of the original twelve disciples only John died a natural death in his old age.

JOHN THE BAPTIST
Matthew 3, 4:12, 11:2-19;
Mark 1:1-11, 6:14-29;
Luke 1, 3:1-22, 9:7-9;
John 1:19-37

"Prepare the way of the Lord!"

This was the task of John the Baptist, son of Zacharias and Elisabeth. He was a powerful preacher in the Judean desert who wore camel skin clothes and ate a diet of locusts and wild honey. People came to John in great numbers and he admonished them to repent and confess their sins, whereupon he baptized them in the River Jordan. Was he the Messiah? they asked. No, he replied. But soon the Messiah would appear and would baptize not with water but with the Holy Spirit.

One day John's cousin Jesus came to be baptized. This, John knew, was the man whose arrival he had predicted. "You should baptize me instead," John protested.

But Jesus reassured him. "This is the way God wants us to do it."

So John baptized Jesus in the river. When the Lord emerged from the water, the Holy Spirit came down from the sky and descended upon Jesus like a dove. A voice from heaven proclaimed, "This is my beloved Son. I am well pleased with Him." Thus began Jesus' ministry.

Shortly afterward John was thrown into prison by King Herod. This occurred because Herodias, Herod's wife, was angry that John had denounced their marriage. She had previously been Herod's brother's wife and John told Herod that he was wrong to take his brother's wife. Herodias wanted John killed but Herod, who feared John's popularity, preserved the prophet's life and merely imprisoned him.

John was unsettled by doubt while in prison and sent this message to Jesus, "Are You really the Messiah?"

"Tell John what you are seeing and hearing," Jesus told John's disciples. "The blind see, the lame walk, those with leprosy are healed, the deaf hear, the dead are raised up, and the poor receive the news of salvation. God will bless those who do not reject Me."

This reassurance came at a critical time because Herodias soon found a way to end John's life. Herodias's daughter danced for Herod and his guests at a birthday celebration. The king was so captivated by this that in a moment of weakness he promised her anything she desired. Prompted by her mother, the girl demanded, "Bring me the head of John the Baptist."

Herod was shocked and distraught but he could not go back on his promise. So the great John the Baptist, forerunner of Jesus Christ, was beheaded to appease a sinful queen.

John's epitaph is Jesus' own words: "What did you go out into the desert to see?...A man dressed in fine clothes? No, those who wear fine clothes are in kings' palaces. Then what did you go out to see? A prophet? Yes, I tell you, and more than a prophet....Among those born of women there has not risen anyone greater than John the Baptist."

JONAH
Jonah

Storms on the Mediterranean Sea can be fearful and none was more ominous than the one that boiled there in 862 B.C. and engulfed a little ship outbound from Joppa.

The vessel rocked dangerously and was deluged by wave after great wave while the crew tossed cargo overboard to lighten the load. They also prayed fervently. But the storm intensified.

They thought that perhaps someone among them had provoked the Lord's wrath and brought on this calamity. Then they remembered the passenger Jonah. They knew he was fleeing from God. Yet he was fast asleep despite the drastic pitching of the vessel. Who was he? What had he done to bring on such terror?

Jonah admitted he was the likely cause of their peril. And he told the crew the solution—throw him into the sea, then the waters would calm. The sailors at first could not bring themselves to do this. They tried to maneuver the ship toward land, but it was futile. So they followed Jonah's brazen advice and cast him into the sea. Immediately the storm abated.

Jonah was a Hebrew prophet. The Lord had commanded that he travel to Nineveh, a huge city on the River Tigris far to the northeast of Judea. There he was to warn the people that their wickedness would soon be punished. It seemed to Jonah that this was a long way to go to for nothing but trouble. So he fled by ship in the opposite direction. Jonah wanted the Lord to find another prophet for this difficult and dangerous mission to Nineveh.

Despite Jonah's attempt to flee from God, his disobedience was used for God's purposes. The experience of the storm and the sudden calming of the waves was such a dramatic demonstration of the Lord's power and grace that the crew of the ship worshipped God and pledged to honor Him.

Meanwhile, God had no intention of letting Jonah off the hook—even by death. So a gigantic fish swallowed the hapless man after he was cast from the ship. For three days the fish swam the sea with Jonah alive in its belly. The wretched prophet prayed for his life and repented, and the Lord heard. At God's command, the leviathan vomited Jonah onto the shore.

Jonah followed God's orders, journeyed to Nineveh, and preached to the people that, because of their sinfulness, their city would be destroyed in forty days. The people listened, stopped their evil ways, and asked the Lord's forgiveness. The Lord forgave them and granted their city a reprieve from judgment.

However, instead of being overjoyed at the Ninevites' change of heart, Jonah was angry. God sent him on this exhausting, dangerous errand, knowing full well that in the end the people would repent and be forgiven! "I want to die," the pitiful Jonah told the Lord. "You care about the wrong things," said the Lord. "It is right for Me to be concerned for a great city like Nineveh."

JONATHAN
1 Samuel 13:3-4; 13:16-14:46; 18:1-4;
19:1-7; 20; 23:16-18; 31:1-5;
2 Samuel 1:1-27

How hard it must be to have a friend who is also your father's enemy—especially if your father is the most powerful man in the country. This was Jonathan's predicament. When the young shepherd David killed Goliath, Saul, king of Israel, brought David into his service. At that time Jonathan, Saul's son, gave David his clothing and armor as tokens and they became loyal friends.

Jonathan's allegiance soon saved David's life. Saul knew the Lord loved David and was afraid God would replace him with the youngster. David won many battles over the Philistines, Israel's great foe, and his popularity disturbed Saul and stirred his jealousy. He became obsessed with the thought of killing David. Jonathan tried to change Saul's mind by gently reminding him of David's invaluable service. Saul agreed not to hurt David—but this promise soon was forgotten.

Saul's anger toward David became uncontrollable so Jonathan stepped in to help David escape. Jonathan knew David was going to become king, and he wanted to serve as David's right-hand man. They swore before God to always be loyal and helpful to each other and to each other's family.

Sadly this was not to be. In a battle against the Philistines at Mount Gilboa, Saul was killed along with Jonathan and two of Saul's other sons. David grieved long for Jonathan and even for the relentless Saul. David wrote "The Song of the Bow" about Saul and Jonathan and required that everyone in Judah learn it. To David, Jonathan was his brother and he lamented the loss of such a faithful friend.

JOSEPH THE SON OF JACOB
Genesis 37, 39-50

W as he arrogant or just sincerely proud? Whichever, Joseph grated on the nerves of his ten older brothers. He clearly was their father's favorite. Jacob had even given him a special gift of a lavishly colored coat.

Not only so, Joseph had the audacity to tell his brothers about his dreams—stories of symbolic bundles of wheat and celestial bodies which implied that the brothers would some day pay Joseph homage.

One day as Joseph's brothers tended sheep, they saw the boy coming across the field. "Here comes that dreamer," they scoffed, and conspired to put an end to Joseph's insolence. They would have killed him but for the mercy of Reuben, their oldest sibling. He proposed they throw him into a dry well. This they did. But when a caravan of Ishmaelites en route to Egypt happened by, they sold Joseph to them as a slave. Thus the lineage of Abraham was diverted to this foreign land.

Although only a slave Joseph prospered in Egypt. His master, Potiphar, the commander of Pharaoh's palace guard, placed Joseph in charge of his entire household. But this favored position was not to last. Potiphar's wife, impressed by the handsome young man, tried to seduce Joseph. When he refused, she connived to have him jailed.

But still the Lord brought Joseph back to prominence, this time through his timely interpretation of Pharaoh's troubling dreams. Joseph told Pharaoh that his dreams indicated there would soon be seven years of abundant crops in Egypt followed by seven years of famine. Pharaoh heeded this warning and stored up reserves of grain for the coming hard times and made Joseph the governor of the whole country—even though he was still a slave!

A dramatic family reunion came when, during the famine, Joseph's brothers journeyed to Egypt to buy food. Of course, they did not recognize Joseph and he played a hard game with them. The youngest brother Benjamin, who was Jacob's favorite, was set up as a thief. This warranted severe punishment in Egypt. But Judah, one of the older brothers, assumed the blame for Benjamin. Joseph was so moved by this that he revealed his identity and tearfully welcomed them. And the brothers paid him homage just as the dreams had said. Jacob's entire household relocated to Egypt during this difficult time and Joseph took care of them.

In time, however, the descendants of Jacob would become slaves of the Egyptians because no one like Joseph remained in power to look after their interests. This set the stage for the dramatic Exodus of the children of Israel and their odyssey to the Promised Land.

JOSEPH THE HUSBAND OF MARY
Matthew 1 and 2; Luke 1:26-56; 2:1-50

Joseph of Nazareth learned that Mary, his betrothed, was expecting a child! He knew this was not his child so naturally he decided to divorce her, though privately so as not to expose her to public disgrace. But in a dream, an angel told Joseph that Mary's baby was conceived by the Holy Spirit and would grow to become the Savior of the world.

So Joseph married Mary. But during the pregnancy, the couple had to travel to Bethlehem in Judea and register their names as part of a census ordered by Augustus Caesar. There was played out the well-known story of the king born in a stable. Joseph named the infant Jesus, as he had been instructed to do. Then he was warned by an angel that Herod the Great was looking for the baby Messiah. So Joseph fled with his family to Egypt where they stayed until Herod died and it was safe for them to return to Nazareth.

Joseph must have wondered how this normal little child could grow to become the Messiah! But when Jesus was twelve Joseph caught a glimpse of Jesus' greatness. As usual, the family went to Jerusalem to celebrate the annual Passover feast. Afterward, on the way home among the throngs of other pilgrims, Mary and Joseph noticed Jesus was not with them. Worried, they turned and hurried back to Jerusalem. There they found Jesus in the temple, of all places, carrying on intelligent discourse with the scholarly teachers!

"Why are You here?" they demanded. "We've been looking everywhere for You."

"Don't you know I need to be here, in My Father's house?" He replied.

But He returned home with them and grew up an obedient boy.

Joseph of Nazareth was given a very special role in history. He struggled as an ordinary father and husband to provide for his family in a captive society. Yet he was the father chosen to provide protection and nurture to the Son of Man.

JOSHUA
Deuteronomy 31:1-8; 34:5-9; Joshua

"Y ou're the one who will lead our people into God's Promised Land."

Those words, spoken by the aging Moses, must have thrilled Joshua's heart—and given him much trepidation. There were strong nations to conquer once the Hebrews crossed the Jordan River. "Do not be afraid," Moses told him. "God Himself will lead you. He will not abandon you."

Israel reached the Jordan near Jericho at flood time. A crossing seemed impossible. But God told Joshua He would perform a miracle to display the fact that God's blessings were with him. And sure enough, when the priests carrying the ark of God's covenant waded into the swollen waters, the river stopped flowing! The people were able to go across the dry river bottom.

One day near Jericho, Joshua encountered an angel with a sword. "Are you friend or foe?" Joshua asked, thinking the angel was human.

"Neither," the angel replied. "I am captain of the Lord's army."

Joshua bowed low to the angel, who commanded him to take off his sandals. "You're standing on holy ground," the angel said.

Joshua may be remembered best for the capture of Jericho. It was a well-guarded city, but the Lord told Joshua it was his for the taking. God's tactic was simple but strange. The Israelite army, led by priests carrying the ark of the covenant, was to march around the city for six days. On the seventh day, the priests were to blow trumpets while soldiers marched around the city seven times. Then as the trumpets sounded one extended note, the soldiers were to shout, and the walls of Jericho would collapse!

In this way Jericho was leveled and its inhabitants annihilated. Joshua placed the Lord's curse on anyone who might try to rebuild the city.

At long last the Israelites settled in Canaan, the Promised Land. Joshua ruled wisely and the Lord sent miracles to help Joshua's army subdue their enemies. Joshua divided the land among the Israelites and renewed their covenant with the Lord. He gave his people a choice: Worship the one true God and be blessed, or keep worthless idols and suffer punishment. "As for my household," said Joshua, "we will serve the Lord."

JUDAS ISCARIOT

Matthew 10:1-4; 26:14-16, 21-25, 45-50; 27:3-10;
Mark 3:13-19; 14:10-11, 18-21, 43-45;
Luke 6:13-16; 22:3-6, 20-23, 47-48;
John 12:1-8; 13:2 18-30; 17:12; 18:1-5;

The other apostles never dreamed one of Jesus' twelve closest followers would conspire to turn Him over to His enemies to be falsely accused, tried, and executed.

Judas Iscariot was chosen by Jesus along with the other apostles to go out and preach for Him. He also served as the disciples' treasurer. But he seems to have placed an emphasis on money rather than devotion. When Mary poured perfume upon the Lord, Judas criticized her. "This perfume should have been sold and the money given to the poor," he said. But Jesus respected Mary's gesture and corrected Judas. "The poor will always be with you," Jesus said, "but I will not always be with you."

At the Last Supper, Jesus predicted that one of the twelve who were eating with Him would betray Him. "Surely it can't be me!" cried Judas, although he already had bargained secretly to turn Jesus over to the chief priests for thirty pieces of silver.

"You have said so," Jesus replied.

Later that night, when Jesus went to pray in the Garden of Gethsemane, Judas appeared with a mob. "Rabbi!" greeted Judas, and kissed his master. The word Rabbi was the code which Judas would use by arrangement to identify Jesus in the darkness.

The mob dragged Jesus away to be tried. But soon Judas heard that Jesus had been given the death sentence. He sorely regretted his betrayal and so took the thirty pieces of silver back to the priests and told them that he had sinned. "Jesus is innocent!" he said. When they refused to listen, Judas threw the money into the temple, went out, and hanged himself.

By law the priests could not put Judas' silver in their treasury—it was blood money. Instead they used it to buy land for a graveyard where nameless strangers could be buried.

LAZARUS
John 11:1-45; 12:1-11, 17-19

Others had performed miracles, but no one except the prophets Elijah and Elisha had ever been known to bring the dead back to life. Yet Jesus knew it was not yet time for His friend Lazarus to leave this world.

Lazarus was a brother of Jesus' followers Mary and Martha. He lived in Bethany. When Jesus heard that Lazarus had become gravely ill, He said that His friend had merely fallen asleep. But Lazarus was indeed dead. He had lain inside a tomb for four days by the time Jesus and His followers drew near Bethany. "If You had been here, he would not have died," Martha and Mary grieved, coming out to meet Jesus.

"He will live again," Jesus said.

He asked to be taken to the cave where Lazarus was

entombed. "Remove the stone," He commanded.

"But he'll be smelling awful," Martha gasped. "He's been dead four days!"

"Believe, and you will see the glory of God," Jesus told her. When the stone had been moved, Jesus prayed aloud that God would perform a miracle here so the people would know that He was God's Son. Then He called into the cave, "Lazarus, come out!"

The man who had died emerged, bound in burial clothes from head to toe.

As a result of Lazarus' resurrection, many doubters started to believe Jesus indeed was the Messiah. This frightened Jesus' opponents and accelerated their efforts to have Him killed.

LOT
Genesis 11:31; 12:4; 13:1-14:16; 19:1-38;
Luke 17:28-30

When God sent Abraham and his wife Sarah into the land of Canaan, they were accompanied by Abraham's nephew Lot. In time, Abraham and Lot prospered in the new land. As their flocks grew larger, however, their shepherds quarreled over pasture land. To make peace, Abraham gave Lot his choice of land to settle on, so Lot moved east to the fertile Jordan River valley. There he pitched his tents near Sodom, a city of evil people. Meanwhile, Abraham settled in Canaan.

Intercity warfare soon visited the Jordan valley and Lot

and his household were taken captive by a conquering army. When Abraham got word of this he took several hundred men and pursued the marauders. In the aftermath of a brilliant surprise attack, Abraham's men scattered the enemy and rescued Lot and the other captives.

Fifteen years later, Lot found himself in even greater trouble. The cities of Sodom and Gomorrah had become so evil that God planned to destroy them. Lot was sitting near the city gate of Sodom when two men (who were actually angels) approached. Lot insisted that they stay with him and share a meal. After supper they were roused to find that Lot's house was surrounded by all the men of the city. The evil men called for Lot to send the two men outside. The mob had wicked intentions. Lot was afraid for the strangers and to pacify the mob offered to send his two virgin daughters out to them. "Do not harm my guests," he pleaded. Lot's refusal to release the strangers to them angered the would-be molesters. They rushed the door of the house, but the two angels struck them blind!

The angels instructed Lot to take his family and leave immediately because the Lord's destruction of Sodom was imminent. Naturally, Lot's family resisted. The angels had to take Lot, his wife, and his two daughters by the hand and lead them out of the city. As they fled in the predawn hour, God rained fiery sulfur down on the cities of Sodom and Gomorrah which were consumed together with all their inhabitants. Lot and his family were saved. All except for Lot's wife. She could not resist turning to look back at the destruction of her home. At that very spot she was turned to a pillar of salt.

This sordid story does not end here. After their escape from Sodom, Lot and his two daughters lived in a cave. The daughters worried that they would never be married and have children. So they made their father drunk and slept with him. The two children which came forth from these incestuous unions were ancestors of the nations of Moab and Ammon, future enemies of Israel.

LUKE
Luke; Acts

Which of the four authors of the Gospels was a medical doctor? Whose meticulous, methodical writing style gives him away? It was Luke.

This thorough biblical writer handed down parables and details about Jesus' life that are found nowhere else. For example, Luke sought to convince readers that Jesus Christ came back to life physically after the Crucifixion. To accomplish this the writer pointed out that the resurrected Savior ate fish with His disciples. This unique bit of evidence emphasizes a physical resurrection.

Luke also wrote the book of Acts as a continuation of his gospel. It chronicles the spread of Christ's church during the first century. Luke accompanied the apostle Paul through Asia and Macedonia. This book of New Testament history shows how the early Christians struggled not only to spread the Gospel, but to understand how the Gospel applied to their world.

Tradition says that Luke met a martyr's death, hanged on an olive tree in Greece.

MARK
Mark; Acts 12:12, 25; 13:5, 13; 15:36-39; Colossians 4:10-11; 2 Timothy 4:11; Philemon 23-24; 1 Peter 5:13

The young disciple Mark was eager to spread the wonderful news of Jesus Christ, especially to the non-Jewish world. His gospel is the shortest of the four, and possibly was the first to be written.

Mark's enthusiasm shows in his action-oriented writing. He skips altogether the story of the Savior's birth and begins his account with Jesus' baptism by John the Baptist at the onset of His ministry. By the end of the first chapter of the Gospel of Mark, Jesus has already resisted Satan, chosen four disciples, and performed many miracles of healing and exorcism.

Mark labored with Paul, Peter, Barnabas, and others to build up the early church. It is thought that Mark was martyred like his fellow workers. According to one account, Mark was dragged to death through the streets of Alexandria.

MATTHEW
Matthew; Mark 2:13-17; 3:13-19;
Luke 5:27-32; 6:12-16;
Acts 1:12-14

A Jewish tax collector was not a desirable companion in first-century Palestine where the Jews lived under bondage to Roman taxes. Yet Matthew was called by Jesus and joined His band of disciples. When the Pharisees demanded to know why Jesus associated with "sinners and tax collectors," Jesus replied, "Those who are well do not need a doctor. I've come to call sinners, not righteous people, to repent."

Matthew wrote an in-depth account of Jesus' life and teachings. Whereas Luke wanted to reach Gentile readers with the good news of Jesus' salvation, Matthew's objective was to convince Jews that Jesus was the Messiah as foretold in the Old Testament.

Matthew's record provides the most thorough version of the Sermon on the Mount. He emphasized Jesus' concern with righteousness and concluded with the commission Jesus gave the disciples just before He ascended into heaven: "Go, make disciples in all the nations,..."

Little is known of Matthew's life. Varying accounts say he died in Ethiopia or Macedonia, possibly of natural causes, possibly by execution.

MOSES
Exodus, Leviticus, Numbers, and Deuteronomy

He was born in the worst of times. Not only were his people, the Hebrews, slaves in Egypt; the Pharaoh had decreed that because the slaves were multiplying so fast, every newborn Hebrew boy must be drowned in the Nile. Therefore, Moses' mother kept him hidden for the first three months of his life. When she could keep him no longer, she set him adrift in a reed basket along the edge of the Nile river. The basket was discovered by Pharaoh's daughter. After Moses' own mother raised him, he was adopted into the royal family.

One day, the young man Moses saw an Egyptian beating a Hebrew slave. Moses rushed to his kinsman's defense and killed the Egyptian. Fearing he would be reported and executed, Moses buried the Egyptian in the sand and fled to the land of Midian. There he married and settled down to work as a shepherd. But God had a very important task in mind for Moses. God's people, the Hebrews, were slaves in Egypt and desperately needed a leader to confront Pharaoh and demand their release.

Moses was quietly tending his father-in-law's livestock on Mount Sinai one day when God appeared to him in a burning bush. God commanded the exile to return to Egypt and lead the Hebrews to freedom.

Moses protested, "Who am I to do this?"

"I will be with you," the Lord replied, and commissioned Moses to go in the name of the great "I Am." Then Moses complained that he was not a good orator. So God agreed to let Aaron, Moses' older brother, be his spokesman. God spoke to Moses and Moses relayed God's messages through Aaron.

Moses and Aaron appeared boldly before Pharaoh. The Lord punished Pharaoh's stubbornness by singular means, and the Hebrews ultimately escaped under the leadership of Moses. The Red Sea waters opened and the people were free. This story is an unparalleled epic. Of equal impact is its sequel: The freed masses were mutinous and contentious. Even Moses' own brother Aaron and his sister Miriam joined in their antics. As this horde wandered toward the Promised Land, God, through Moses, gave them the Ten Commandments and other laws.

Moses was faithful to the Lord. But there was an occasion in the Zin Desert when Moses disobeyed the Lord. This failure bred disrespect for God among the people so God did not allow Moses to enter Canaan, the land he had promised to Israel. Before Moses died, however, God let him glimpse the land from the top of Mount Nebo across the Jordan River from Canaan. So Moses died in Moab, and his successor Joshua led the Hebrews into Canaan.

NATHAN

2 Samuel 7:1-17; 12:1-15, 24-25;
1 Kings 1:10-45;
1 Chronicles 17:1-15; 29:29; 2 Chronicles 9:29; 29:25

"Why have you trampled on the Lord's laws and done this evil?" said the prophet to the king. This booming indictment came in response to a serious deed that called into question the sinner's regard for God Almighty. Few people would have the nerve to talk to a king this way. But Nathan the prophet knew that the sin of King David was so great the hills would have roared in anguish had it gone unreproved.

David fell in love with Bathsheba, the wife of a Hittite warrior named Uriah who fought in David's army. Not only so, David had committed adultery with Bathsheba. To lawfully remove Bathsheba's husband so he could marry her, David ordered Joab, the commander of his army, to place Uriah in the thick of battle. Then, to make doubly sure Uriah died, David had his general arrange for the army to withdraw suddenly and leave Uriah alone against the enemy. This was nothing short of murder. After Uriah's death, David took the widow Bathsheba for his wife.

The prophet Nathan became aware of the king's sinfulness and soon arrived in the palace to tell David this story: A rich man owned many cows and sheep. In the same town a poor man lived who owned just one little lamb. The lamb meant a lot to the poor man and his family. In fact, it was their pet. One day the rich man began to prepare a banquet, but he did not want to kill any of his own animals for the meal. So he stole the poor man's lamb, cooked it, and served it to his guests.

David was furious at the fictitious rich man. Then Nathan interpreted, "You are that rich man."

Nathan told David that because of his bloody treachery with Uriah and Bathsheba, David's own family would reap a bloody reward. "This will never again be a peaceful house," Nathan promised.

David repented, and the Lord did not punish him by death. But the newborn son, conceived in David and Bathsheba's adultery, did not live.

NEBUCHADNEZZAR
Daniel 1-4

It took a lot of convincing for King Nebuchadnezzar of Babylon to decide to worship God. He reigned during the sixth and seventh centuries B.C. at the time Jerusalem was captured. Daniel and his colleagues, carried into captivity by the Babylonian army, were trained for royal service. In time, they were given important managerial positions under Nebuchadnezzar. Daniel in particular became indispensable to the king because he was able to interpret Nebuchadnezzar's strange dreams. The king respected Daniel and the others, but he gave little thought to their God.

When Shadrach, Meshach and Abednego refused to worship Nebuchadnezzar's golden idol, he had them thrown into a fiery furnace. They survived and emerged unsinged, as if nothing had happened. The king was amazed and promoted them to more powerful positions, but still he declined to worship their God.

But the Lord in His Kindness reached out to Nebuchadnezzar. As He so often does, God used affliction to draw the king to Him. God took away Nebuchadnezzar's kingdom and power for seven years. Nebuchadnezzar later described himself as living like a wild animal during that time. Some students of Scripture believe this was a result of an hallucination or mental derangement. Whatever the condition, Nebuchadnezzar at last prayed to Daniel's God. He was healed and restored to power.

Nebuchadnezzar gave this testimony of praise: "Glorify the King in heaven, for He is truthful and fair, and He humiliates the proud." Clearly, God had struck a nerve in Nebuchadnezzar when he demonstrated that He was Lord even over that which matters most to a king—his royal pride.

NOAH
Genesis 5:28-10:32

Judgment was at hand. Since the time of Adam and Eve, humans had multiplied, spread across the earth, and progressively turned away from God. "I am sorry I created them," God said of these violent and wicked people. "I will destroy every living creature on the face of the earth."

Only one man feared and obeyed God. His name was Noah. God told him of His plan to destroy both humans and animals with a great flood. But God gave Noah specific instructions for building an ark in which he, his family, and two each of every living creature would ride out the deluge.

The ark was like a huge barge, one hundred-and-fifty yards long and three stories high. Noah followed every detail of the Lord's commands, built the ark of strong wood, and sealed it carefully with pitch.

Finally the ark was finished. God gave Noah seven days to gather and board all of the animals. Then He made it rain forty days and nights. The flood rose, covered the lowlands, then the hills, and finally even the highest mountains. The water was so deep that once the rain stopped, five months passed before flood receded and the ark came to rest in the mountains of Ararat. It was many more months before the earth was dry again. Noah waited inside the ark until God told him to leave the ark.

The first thing Noah did was make an offering of one of each of the sacrificial animals that had been in the ark. The Lord was pleased by this offering and promised Noah He never again would destroy every living creature. A rainbow appeared in the sky as a perpetual reminder of this covenant with Noah. God gave Noah dominion over all the animals and plants. Everyone living on the earth today is descended from Noah and his sons Shem, Ham, and Japheth.

PAUL

Acts 7:57-28:30; The Letters of Paul

When Stephen, the first Christian martyr, was stoned to death in Jerusalem, a young man named Saul kept the coats of the men who attacked him. Saul then joined the general effort to eradicate Christ's disciples and became one of the leading persecutors of the early church. He went from house to house, arrested the believers, and threw them in jail.

The Jewish leaders sent Saul to Damascus to arrest Christ's followers there. But on the way Saul met Jesus. This would have enormous impact on the spread of Christianity.

On the road to Damascus, the Lord appeared to Saul and his companions as a blinding light. "Why are you persecuting Me?" a voice demanded.

"Who are You?" Saul asked.

"It is Me, Jesus, the One you are persecuting."

Blinded and trembling, Saul asked, "What do You want me to do?"

Jesus told him to go into Damascus and wait for instructions there.

Meanwhile the Lord told a believer in Damascus named Ananias to find Saul. Ananias was hesitant because he'd heard of Saul's merciless persecution of the Christians. But he did as God told him.

When Ananias touched Saul, scales fell from the tormentor's eyes so he could see again. Right away Saul was baptized and filled with the Holy Spirit, joined the believers in Damascus, and began preaching with power that astonished the hearers. They knew he'd come to Damascus as an enemy of Christ, not a believer. Not only so, the Jewish leaders there conspired to kill him. But his Christian friends smuggled him out of the city hidden in a large basket.

Saul returned to Jerusalem. At first, he was rejected by the Christians because of his reputation. They doubted that their former persecutor had sincerely believed in Christ. But through the mediation of a church leader named Barnabas, Saul was accepted and began to help build up the young church. Again the Jewish leaders tried to kill him, and again his new Christian comrades whisked him away to safety.

Saul became a missionary and soon after became known as Paul. He and his companions traveled through the Roman Empire preaching the gospel, encouraging new believers, and teaching the young churches how to worship and conduct their lives as believers. Paul and his companions were the objects of harassment and imprisonment and ultimately were executed for their beliefs. This was a complete role reversal for the one-time persecutor named Saul.

In his journeys through the eastern Mediterranean, Paul lived in constant danger from the Lord's foes and from the uncertainties of travel. Not only was he shipwrecked, he was jailed and often beaten.

Even in captivity Paul was a powerful witness for Christ. Once Paul and his companion Silas were imprisoned in Philippi because they freed a slave girl from an evil spirit of fortune-telling. Her owners were furious with Paul and Silas because the owners had been using her fortune-telling as a means of making money. They convinced the court to imprison Paul.

Stripped and severely beaten, Paul and Silas were chained deep inside the prison. There, in the middle of the night, the apostles prayed and sang hymns to the other prisoners! Next, God sent an earthquake that shook the prison so violently that the heavy doors fell open and the chains were loosened from the inmates. When the jailer ran to investigate, he thought the prisoners had escaped. The Romans would kill him for this! He was about to commit suicide when Paul stopped him. "Don't worry," Paul told him, "We are all here." The jailer and his entire household believed in Jesus as a result of this event.

Paul was finally sent to Rome for a trial before Caesar Nero. While awaiting trial, Paul continued to preach the Gospel for two years while living in a rented house. Scripture does not record his end, but it's assumed that Paul was beheaded in Rome before Nero fell from power in A.D. 68.

PETER
Matthew, Mark; Luke; John;
Acts 1-5; 9-12; 1 Peter; 2 Peter

Simon Peter was introduced to Jesus Christ by his brother Andrew. Jesus told the brawny fisherman, "You will be named Cephas," a name which means "a stone."

Peter was involved in one of the Savior's first miracles. Jesus had been preaching from Peter's fishing boat to the multitudes gathered along the shore of the Sea of Galilee. When He finished speaking, Jesus told Peter to row into deep water and let down his fishing nets.

"But there are no fish here," Peter complained wearily. "We've been fishing all night and we've caught nothing."

But he did as Jesus suggested—and caught so many fish that his nets started breaking. His partners came to help and they pulled up so many fish their boats started to sink.

Awestruck by Jesus' power, Peter fell at His feet. "Stay away from me," Peter told Him. "I'm a terrible sinner."

Jesus already knew this and it did not affect His plans for Peter. "I'm going to make you a fisher of men," Jesus told him. After Jesus' Resurrection and Ascension, Peter was leader of the early church. He was a simple, seemingly impulsive man who did not consider the consequences of his words and deeds.

Peter must have been shaken to his sandals when at the Last Supper Jesus said, "Simon, Satan has asked to sift you like wheat. I have prayed that you will remain faithful." Peter could not imagine what perils Jesus referred to, but he was confident that he would follow the Lord anywhere. "I am even ready to die with you," Peter promised. Jesus corrected him. "Before the rooster crows in the morning, you will deny me three times."

When Jesus was arrested in the garden, Peter tried to defend Him and struck one of the assailants with his sword, cutting off an ear. Jesus admonished Peter to put away his weapon, and with a touch healed the wounded man. Shortly afterward, Jesus was taken into custody in a house. Peter stayed outside warming himself around a fire. A servant girl asked, "Weren't you one of his followers?"

"I do not know him," Peter replied impulsively, fearing

for his own safety. Twice more during the next hour, Peter was openly suspected of following Jesus. Both times Peter repeated his denial.

It's sad that the triple denial comes to mind when Peter's name is mentioned because Peter truly became a stone built into the spiritual house which is the church of God.

PHILIP
Matthew 10:1-4; Mark 3:13-19; Luke 6:12-16;
John 1:43-51; 6:5-7; 12:20-22; 14:8-14

One of the first evangelists on record was the apostle Philip. Soon after he was called by Jesus, he told the skeptic Nathaniel, "We've found the one Moses and the prophets were writing about! He's Jesus of Nazareth."

"Can anything good come out of Nazareth?" Nathaniel grumbled.

There must have been a twinkle in Philip's eye when he replied, "Come see."

And Nathaniel followed the Lord.

Before miraculously feeding the five thousand at the Sea of Galilee, Jesus likewise must have had a twinkle in His eye when He turned to Philip and asked "Where can we get enough bread for all these people to eat?"

Philip shook his head in dismay. "Six months' pay wouldn't buy even a sampling for this many people."

Jesus took all the available food—five loaves of bread and a couple of fish—and turned it into a feast.

Still Philip needed reminding. At the Last Supper, Jesus told His disciples, "No one can come to the Father except through Me."

"Lord, show us the Father," Philip requested. "Then we'll be convinced of what You say."

"Philip, have I been with You all this time, and you still do not know Me?" Jesus answered. "Believe that I am in the Father, and the Father in Me. If you cannot believe My words, then believe because of the miracles you have seen Me perform."

Philip did believe, and helped spread the gospel after Jesus' Resurrection and Ascension. He is thought to have been martyred in Asia Minor.

PONTIUS PILATE
Matthew 27:1-2, 11-31; Mark 15:1-20;
Luke 3:1; 23:1-25; John 18:28-19:22

Pontius Pilate was the Roman governor of Palestine in the time of Christ. The last thing he wanted to deal with was some explosively sensitive, incomprehensible altercation among the Jews in Jerusalem. But he was charged with hearing and judging local disputes.

One such dispute raged between the Jewish leaders and Jesus of Nazareth. Jesus was arrested and dragged before Pilate early one the morning. Pilate heard the case and questioned Jesus. He was very surprised that Jesus did not respond to the accusations of the chief priests and elders of the Jewish people. He could find nothing that Jesus had done wrong. When Pilate learned that Jesus was a Galilean, he tried to defer judgment to King Herod who happened to be in Jerusalem at the time. But Herod and his men merely beat and mocked Jesus and sent Him back to Pilate.

Pilate had a diplomatic way out of this mess. He had a custom of releasing a prisoner at the time of the Jewish Passover each year and had in custody a particularly troublesome criminal named Barabbas. "I can give you Barabbas, or I can give you Jesus," Pilate told the people gathered at Jesus' trial. He hoped the crowd would pick Jesus to be released. Then he would not have to deal with the chief priests' claim. But the mob had been stirred up by the Jewish elders. They picked the dreadful Barabbas to be set free.

Pilate's wife had had a very disturbing dream about Jesus. "Have nothing to do with that Man," she warned. But Pilate had to do his duty. He asked the mob again whether they wanted him to release Jesus or the criminal Barabbas. "Give us Barabbas!" they demanded. So Pilate washed his hands in front of everyone, meaning that he considered himself free from blame if the innocent man was executed. "Kill Him yourselves," he told the Jewish leaders.

To Pilate, the judgment of Jesus Christ was a harrying annoyance. It may have been a dramatic incident, but at the time he basically regarded his role in one of the most important events in the history of civilization as little more than a distraction from his routine duties.

SAMSON

Judges 13-16

Today's superheroes of sports are weaklings compared to a real hero who lived three thousand years ago. When Samson flexed his muscles, heavy cords snapped like rotten string. He once slew a thousand enemies using the jawbone of an ass for a weapon. He uprooted the gates of the city of Gaza and carried them to the top of a distant hill. When attacked by a lion, he made no attempt to escape or tame the animal; with his bare hands he tore its jaws apart! How many of our professional football stars—or entire championship teams—do you suppose would attempt that?

Samson's feats were the work of the Lord. The Spirit of God came over him and suddenly he was empowered with incredible strength.

Samson was a Hebrew judge during the years when God allowed the Israelites to fall captive to the Philistines. The wife of the Israelite Manoah learned from an angel of the Lord she would give birth to a son who would rescue the Jews from their captors. When Samson was born, the Holy Spirit came upon him and he grew to become the Philistines' terror. On one occasion he killed thirty of them. Another time he caught three hundred foxes, tied torches to their tails, and ran them through the Philistines' fields, thus causing their crops to burn. After slaughtering more Philistines, Samson went into the wilderness and lived in a cave.

At one point Samson let himself be captured and turned over to the Philistines. But when his enemies began to celebrate his capture, he snapped his bonds and massacred them.

The Philistines finally found a way to contain him. He fell in love with a woman named Delilah. The Philistine leaders offered her an enormous sum of money if she could find out the source of Samson's strength. Samson treated Delilah's nagging about his strength as a game. "Tie me up with seven unseasoned bow strings," he told her. "That will normalize my power." Delilah tied him up and summoned the Philistines to come for him. But when he saw them, Samson immediately broke free.

"New ropes will do it," he teased. "Tie me in ropes that have never been used."

Again she tied him, and again he broke his bonds.

Samson had long, wavy hair that had never been cut. "Weave my hair in your loom," he said, "and I'll be as weak as any other man." But again, when Delilah thought she and her conspirators had him at bay, Samson laughingly broke away.

At last he told her the true secret of his strength. "I was dedicated to God when I was born," he said, "so my hair has never been cut. My hair is the key to my strength." Soon Delilah sang him softly to sleep and cut his hair. When he awoke and tried to summon his strength, he found that the Spirit had left him. He was captured. The Philistines put out his eyes, bound him in chains, and threw him in prison where he was forced to grind their grain.

Later the inebriated Philistines were at a festival in honor of their pagan god. They called for Samson to be brought from the dungeon into their temple so they could mock him publicly. Several thousand people were gathered to taunt the once-proud Israelite. But Samson's hair had grown back. He slyly persuaded his guard to position his hands for him between the two main pillars of the temple. Then he prayed that God would strengthen him for one last mighty feat.

God answered his prayer. Samson pushed against the great pillars as hard as he could, they gave way, the temple collapsed on the hordes of Philistine mockers—and on Samson. It is recorded that he killed more Philistines with his last act than he had killed in all his other deeds combined.

SAMUEL
1 and 2 Samuel

Eli the high priest was almost blind when he was given a little boy named Samuel to raise in Shiloh. Samuel served him well, but Eli's own sons—priests like their father— were selfish and disrespectful of God. God determined to punish the family.

One night while Samuel was sleeping, the Lord called him by name. Samuel thought the voice he heard must be Eli's, so he rose and went to Eli's bedside. "What do you need?" he asked the priest.

"I didn't call you," Eli said grumpily. "Go back to sleep."

After Samuel had settled into his bedding, the Lord called his name again. Again he went to Eli and asked, "What do you want?" And again the agitated priest sent Samuel back to bed.

When it happened a third time and Samuel appeared at his bedside, Eli realized God was calling Samuel. "Go back to bed," Eli told him. "If you hear the voice, say, 'I hear you, Lord. What do you want?'"

Samuel did as he was told and the Lord gave him a dreadful message. God said that Eli and his family were going to be punished forever because of the disrespect of Eli's sons. Understandably, Samuel did not want to share this news with his mentor. But Eli demanded to know what God had said to him. So Samuel relayed the prophecy to him.

"He is God," Eli acknowledged sadly. "He will do the right thing."

As Samuel grew to manhood, God appeared to him with more messages. The people realized Samuel was God's prophet. In fact, Samuel became the last great judge of the Israelites.

Samuel made judges of his own sons. But like the sons of Eli, they were ungodly. The Israelites did not want to follow them, and they demanded that Samuel in his old age appoint a king to rule the nation. This was not what the Lord wanted. Samuel warned them but they insisted. So Samuel anointed a king for them. His name was Saul.

For a time, Saul was a good leader who protected his people. But eventually he turned away from God. Then God told Samuel, "I'm sorry I made Saul king of my people." He sent Samuel to the house of Jesse to find another king. Jesse's youngest son David would become Israel's greatest leader, but he was just a boy when Samuel privately anointed him to succeed the reigning King Saul.

SAUL
1 Samuel 9-31

The young man Saul, son of Kish, was a head taller than any other Israelite. This handsome young man was introduced to Samuel, the prophet/judge who would bring him to power. Saul and his servant were looking for some escaped donkeys and were on the verge of giving up. The servant suggested they find the prophet Samuel and see if he could point them to their donkeys.

Samuel did much more than that. With a jar of olive oil, he anointed Saul king of the land! The Holy Spirit took hold of Saul and he danced and shouted.

At first, Saul diligently sought the Lord's guidance and victoriously led the Israelites into battle against their enemies. But on one critical occasion, he failed to follow God's instructions carefully and it cost him his kingship.

Samuel told Saul that God wanted to punish the Amalekites for their past opposition to the Hebrews. "Attack them and destroy them," Samuel ordered the king. "Leave none of them, young or old, alive. Kill even the babies. Kill all their domestic animals, too."

Saul's soldiers attacked and slaughtered the Amalekites and took their king prisoner. But Saul failed to carry out God's command. He let the heathen king live. Moreover, his men killed only the weakest sheep and cattle and held back the choicest livestock, ostensibly to offer as sacrifices to the Lord.

God was very displeased with Saul. He had given Saul victory over Israel's longtime enemy and Saul had responded with disobedience. God sent Samuel to inform the king that God hereby rejected him. God then sent the prophet to secretly anoint David as the future successor.

Saul brought the youthful David into his service as a court musician. David soon won the heart of the nation in his famous encounter with the Philistine giant Goliath. Saul became paranoid and jealous of David. He sensed that the young man might take his place and wanted to kill him. Soon, David and his growing legions of followers were driven into exile by King Saul.

Interestingly, it wasn't David or any of his men who ultimately ended Saul's life. In fact, David on more than one occasion let Saul live when he easily could have killed his tormentor. Rather Saul and his sons died in a battle against Israel's fierce rivals, the Philistines. Although it brought his persecution to an end, Saul's death did not make David happy. Rather he wrote a heartrending lament for Saul.

SOLOMON
1 Kings 1-11; Proverbs; Ecclesiastes;
the Song of Solomon

God spoke to the new king in a dream, "Tell Me what

you wish." The king was already awed by the enormity of his new responsibility. He realized that he was very young to be the ruler of Israel. "Give me wisdom," he prayed, "so I can rule wisely and always know right from wrong." God was pleased with this humble, mature request. "I will make you wiser than anyone who has ever lived or anyone yet to be born," He promised.

This new king was Solomon, son of David. Early in his reign he had the opportunity to display this God-given wisdom. Two women who lived in the same house each had an infant son. One of the babies was accidentally smothered to death, and both women claimed to be the mother of the surviving child. They appeared before the king for a judgment.

"Bring a sword and cut the living child in half," Solomon ordered. "Give each woman a half of the child."

"No! Please don't kill him!" one of the women cried. "Let her take him!"

Solomon knew immediately this was the child's true mother. She loved the baby so much she was willing to surrender him rather than see him killed. He restored the infant to her. This deepened the king's respect among the people.

Solomon built and furnished a majestic temple to God's honor in Jerusalem and Israel prospered greatly. This temple was the one his father David had desired to build. Solomon built a beautiful, ornate palace for himself. Even today people know of the wealth of Solomon. He recognized that this wealth came from God and prayed for the Lord's blessings over the Israelites.

Although wealth did not corrupt him—at least, not directly

—his lust for women did. The Bible says that Solomon had seven hundred wives and three hundred mistresses. Many of them were foreigners from the lands of Israel's enemies. God had forbidden the Israelites to intermarry. Predictably, some of these wives and concubines persuaded the aging king to worship their own heathen gods.

Solomon's sinful ways soon would be punished by civil war among the Hebrew tribes. Despite all this, because of his love for Solomon's father David, God pledged to let Solomon remain in power until the day he died.

STEPHEN
Acts 6:5-8:2

He had a face like an angel as the false case was brought against him. Stephen, chosen to serve the church in Jerusalem, was charged with preaching against the law of Moses and against God. In reality, Stephen possessed special God-given powers to perform miracles and to speak with wisdom in the name of Christ. He was such an effective speaker that his critics were unable to argue with him. So they plotted lies against him and brought him before the high priest.

When he was asked to defend himself, Stephen spoke eloquently of how God had guided their ancestors. He reminded his listeners how the people of old had revolted against their leader Moses and had angered the Lord by worshipping a idol. He concluded by boldly charging his accusers with breaking Moses' law themselves—and of murdering the Lamb of God, Jesus Christ.

This infuriated them. They became so angry they ground their teeth and covered their ears so they could no longer hear Stephen. A maddened, unreasonable mob finally rushed and seized Stephen.

The brave disciple seemed oblivious to the uproar around him. He lifted his eyes and gazed on a most beautiful vision: the Son of Man, Jesus Christ, standing at the right side of God.

Stephen described what he saw to his tormentors, but it only angered them further. They hustled him outside the city and began throwing rocks at him. Under the deadly barrage, Stephen asked God to receive his spirit. As he fell to his knees, he cried out—as his Savior on the cross had cried out not long before—"Lord, do not count this sin against them." Then he died.

Thus Stephen became the first martyr for Christ. Among the throng of killers was a young man named Saul who became the most dreaded persecutor of the early church—until his own encounter with the Lord changed him into a stead-fast, unflinching Christian martyr like his forerunner, Stephen.

Thomas

Matthew 10:1-4; Mark 3:13-19; Luke 6:12-16;
John 11:14-16; 14:1-7; 20:24-29; Acts 1:12-14

Thomas seems to have been a wet blanket over the joy Jesus spread throughout the land.

When Jesus announced to His disciples they must go to Bethany where their friend Lazarus had just died, Thomas remarked sarcastically, "Yes, let's all go there and die." At the Last Supper, Jesus assured His apostles He was going to prepare a place for them in the Father's house, and they knew the way to follow him there. Thomas challenged, "How can we know the way, since we don't even know where You are going?"

And in the aftermath of the Crucifixion, when Jesus appeared to His followers, Thomas did not believe their reports of seeing the Master. He would not believe, he vowed, unless he could actually touch the nail-scarred palms and put his hand in the Lord's wounded side. Later Jesus entered the locked room where the disciples were staying, and He showed Thomas the pierced hands and had him feel the wound.

"My Lord and my God!" Thomas cried.

"You believe because you have seen Me," Jesus said. "Blessed are those who believe without seeing."

Thomas joined his colleagues in spreading the good news. Yet still today a skeptic is called a doubting Thomas. But Thomas is an important example to us. All the objective evidence in the world could not convince Thomas that

Jesus Christ had risen from the dead. It wasn't enough to be told of the Resurrection—not even by his most trusted friends. Thomas had to see Jesus for himself. He had to have a personal encounter with the Savior. And so it has always been for Christ's believers.

TIMOTHY
Acts 16:1; 17:14-15, 18:5; Philippians 1:1; 2:19;
Colossians 1:1; 1 Timothy; 2 Timothy; Hebrews 13:23

Timothy was Paul's trusted associate—a remarkable status for a young man. He was among the first Christian missionaries, and was in charge of the church in Ephesus on the coast of Asia Minor. Ephesus had been the scene of a major riot when Timothy visited the city with Paul. Like many other leaders of the early church, Timothy endured persecution and imprisonment.

Paul's first letter to Timothy gave advice and instructions on how to lead a church. Paul warned against unsound teachers, discussed the purpose of worship and the necessary qualities of church elders and deacons, admonished Timothy to use his God-given talents, and advised him how to deal with specific problems and circumstances he would face as a church leader. "Don't be self-conscious about your youthfulness," Paul told Timothy. "Just concentrate on setting a good example by what you say, how you live, your love for people, and your faith in God."

Timothy's second letter from Paul was brief and climaxed

with Paul's premonition of his martyrdom. "I have fought the good fight," Paul wrote. "I have finished the race. I have kept the faith."

Paul was in Rome awaiting his trial before Nero when he wrote the letters to Timothy. He implored Timothy and the apostle Mark to join him in Rome. And so perhaps Timothy was present at the martyrdom of the apostle Paul, his father in the faith.

ZACCHEUS
Luke 19:1-10

This little man had a big job: He was chief tax collector in Jericho. This made him both rich and despised because he collected taxes from the common people to give to Rome. Yet even he was interested in the famous teacher and healer from Nazareth.

Jesus was coming into the city. Zaccheus struggled to catch a glimpse of Him through the throng of people. But he was too short to see anything. So he ran ahead of the procession and climbed up a sycamore tree beside the road. From here he could see everyone—and everyone could see him.

Jesus stopped beneath the tree. "Come down, Zaccheus," the Master called. "I'm coming to stay at your house today."

The crowd thought it strange that Jesus would associate with someone they considered a sinner. But while Jesus was at his house Zaccheus changed their minds. He announced he would give half his possessions to the poor and return four times the amount of money he had collected dishonestly.

"Salvation has come to this house today," Jesus said and reminded His critics, "I came to seek and to save those who are lost."

ZECHARIAH
Zechariah; Matthew 26:31

Rejoice, Jerusalem!
Shout, Jerusalem!
Your King is coming.
He is righteous, and He brings salvation.
He is gentle, and He rides on the foal of a donkey. . . .

Thus Zechariah predicted the coming of Jesus Christ, more than five hundred years before His birth. The Jews had returned from captivity in Babylon and began rebuilding the temple and the city of Jerusalem. Zechariah spoke not only of their labors in Jerusalem but of things to come as well. These include the punishment of Israel's ungodly leaders and of the nation's enemies, the coming of the Messiah, the people's repentance from their idolatrous ways, the Lord's final victory over His enemies, and the millennial kingdom.

Jesus Himself referred to Zechariah's prophecy during the Last Supper. "Tonight," He told His disciples, "all of you will stumble because of Me." Then He quoted Zechariah: "Kill the Shepherd and the sheep will scatter."

Zechariah's prophecies serve as stern, necessary warnings to wayward people. They are also words of hope, and vital connectors from Old Testament history to Jesus Christ, and to the building of His glorious church.

Inspirational Library

Beautiful purse/pocket size editions of Christian classics bound in flexible leatherette. These books make thoughtful gifts for everyone on your list, including yourself!

The Bible Promise Book   Over 1000 promises from God's Word arranged by topic. What does God promise about matters like: Anger, Illness, Jealousy, Love, Money, Old Age, and Mercy? Find out in this book!
Flexible Leatherette $3.97

Daily Light   One of the most popular daily devotionals with readings for both morning and evening.
Flexible Leatherette $4.97

Wisdom from the Bible   Daily thoughts from Proverbs which communicate truths about ourselves and the world around us.
Flexible Leatherette $4.97

My Daily Prayer Journal   Each page is dated and features a Scripture verse and ample room for you to record your thoughts, prayers, and praises. One page for each day of the year.
Flexible Leatherette $4.97

Available wherever books are sold.
Or order from:

Barbour & Company, Inc.
P.O. Box 719
Uhrichsville, OH 44683
http://www.barbourbooks.com

If you order by mail add $2.00 to your order for shipping.
Prices subject to change without notice.